SHE EXPLORES

She Explores

Stories of Life-Changing Adventures
on the Road and in the Wild

Gale Straub

CHRONICLE BOOKS
SAN FRANCISCO

Library of Congress Cataloging-in-Publication Data is available.

ISBN 978-1-4521-6766-4

Manufactured in China.

Design by Anne Kenady Smith.

10 9 8 7 6 5 4

Chronicle Books LLC
680 Second Street
San Francisco, California 94107

www.chroniclebooks.com

FOR THOSE WHO PREFER TO
TAKE THE BACK ROADS HOME

BEGINNINGS

Who do you picture when you think
of an outdoorswoman?

What clothes does she wear?

What vehicle does she drive? Does she live in
it? Does she pull a tent out of the back,
arranging it under the stars?

MAYBE SHE'S A REALIST, MAYBE SHE'S A
dreamer. Maybe she's an artist and the varying landscapes she crosses inspire creativity within her. Or maybe the changing landscapes are overwhelming at times. She wants to slow down and stay awhile.

Perhaps she has a family. She's a mother, orienting her children to the world so they can figure out how to orient themselves on their own one day.

Or her children are all grown up, their compasses set. Her time is suddenly all her own.

She's a biologist, a wilderness ranger, a computer programmer.

She's grieving: a loved one, a relationship, a piece of herself.

Maybe she's working tirelessly to share the stories of others. Or perhaps she's articulating her own.

When you imagine this woman, do you see yourself in her? The outdoors is so special because it does not cultivate an archetype for the outdoorswoman. And while society is always tempted to shape us in its image, to create an "ideal" way to look and love and be, on our best days, when we're out there alone in nature, we get the opportunity to define ourselves. Do you see all the possibilities for your own life?

I grew up in a small town in New Hampshire. My earliest outdoor memories include digging up potatoes in my dad's garden and tromping through the woods with my twin sister and older brother. We didn't travel a whole lot, but my dad took us on winding drives through our small state. We were encouraged to peek over stone walls and take the back roads home. My mother is an artist. She turns her interior world inside out by experimenting with new mediums: textiles, pastels, watercolor, pen and ink. My parents instilled in me a quiet curiosity and I'm grateful for that.

In college, I wouldn't have identified as an outdoorswoman, even as I spent weekends hiking in the White Mountains and found solace on long winter walks through the city streets of Boston. I had no sense of who I was or what I wanted from work or relationships, but the time I spent in motion, in open air—that's when I felt most at ease with myself. The pleasure I took from spending time outside was magnified by a deep appreciation for its beauty. Using my dad's old 35 mm Pentax camera, I began taking photographs on those long walks and watching them come to life in the campus darkroom.

I graduated from college in 2008, a turbulent time in the American economy. Aimlessly armed with a psychology degree, I applied to grad school for a crash course in accounting and finance. From there I spent several years working at a "Big Four" accounting firm and then a venture capital firm in Boston. I enjoyed the stability of this work and the direction that came with it. I love problem solving, and accounting has it in spades. In my free time, I continued to hike New Hampshire's worn trails. I escaped to Maine to swim in its clear, deep lakes. And almost every night I wandered my neighborhood with a camera, capturing shadows and bright spots.

By 2013 I'd lived in Boston for almost ten years, and I was starting to feel restless. In certain ways I was lonely, too. I lacked community, like-minded people whom I could share my interests and curiosities with.

Craving new landscapes and adventure, I made the decision with my partner, Jon, to travel in a Sprinter van for a year. We owned no house, had no kids. The timing felt right for us. I saved

for more than fifteen months, and with careful planning, I was fortunate to be able to save money beyond my student loans and rent. I was nervous before we left. I was leaving behind my profession and I was only in my late twenties. As I packed, my landlady, a conservative woman in her sixties, asked me what neighborhood I was moving to. Hesitantly, I told her that I was going to road-trip with Jon.

Her response surprised me: "My husband was a taxi driver. He was happiest behind the wheel. When he retired, we were going to travel the country together in an RV. He died right after he retired. It was so unexpected. Good for you for doing it now. You never know what's going to happen."

We weren't retiring, but I took her sentiment to heart.

I learned so much about myself during those months on the road. I redefined my boundaries. I discovered that I'm bad at recognizing what I need. I moved too fast and my camera shutter released too slowly. Sometimes the blurry images I took mimicked my headspace. At first I was afraid of almost everything, but slowly I found myself exchanging fear for confidence. I cultivated my most intimate relationship in a small space. I traced the Pacific and the Atlantic coasts by road.

My respect for the outdoors grew, as did my interest in trying new, adventurous activities. I hiked South Sister, the third-highest mountain in Oregon, and marveled at how thin the air feels above ten thousand feet. I floated on a surfboard in salt water off Los Angeles and tried to catch a wave. Day by day, I found myself a

little less inhibited. When the trip ended and I returned to New England, I brought that feeling with me.

I started She-Explores.com when we set off on the road trip in 2014. My vision was to create a content site for and about inquisitive women in the outdoors and on the road. The inspiration for the site was multifold. In preparation for our trip, I'd searched the Internet and social media, but I couldn't find many resources for women like me. I had all this pent-up creative energy that I'd harnessed in photographs that I wasn't sharing with anyone. I wanted to find a community of women who love the outdoors and its beauty as much as I do, so I created a platform that allowed women to share their work and their thoughts with others. I hoped to grow an audience that cares about each other and celebrates our successes.

From the beginning, I knew my story wasn't enough to fill the site. I researched and reached out to women who were inspired by time spent outside. I connected with writers, artists, photographers, and fellow travelers. I wanted to hear women's stories, stories that historically have not been highlighted as often as men's.

At first, the site and the stories were largely aesthetic, shaped by the romantic pull of the outdoors. But over time, I learned more about the outdoor space and its political and social nuances. Women actively carved a place for themselves within the outdoor industry by starting their own companies and spearheading grassroots organizations. The essays I received grew more reflective. They were honest and revealing, indicative of the transformative power of nature. After two years, I extended this vision to a *She Explores* podcast. It's allowed me to have dynamic conversations about diversity, hiking solo, mental health, adventuring with kids, conservation, and more. After three years, I collaborated with the thoughtful Laura

Hughes to start a second podcast, *Women on the Road,* which highlights life on the road from the feminine perspective. Audio is an intimate medium; I'm grateful for the women who choose to share their personal stories of adventure, creativity, hardship, and growth with me.

To date, She-Explores.com has featured hundreds of women and highlighted the myriad of ways they experience the outdoors. And it's thrilling to imagine how many more of us are out there.

This book is a compendium of curious, creative outdoorswomen and travelers. I've divided the collection into groups: enthusiasts, creatives, founders and professionals, nomads, transplants, and advocates. But I recognize that we are not one thing; each woman featured is entirely herself, and yet there are overlaps in their interests. She can be a conservationist and an artist. She can be an accountant and a thru-hiker. She can be a climber, a writer, and a traveler. I like to think of the overlaps as the connections between us.

In addition to the personal stories from remarkable women, I share some of my own lessons from time spent in the outdoors and on the road. In the following pages you'll find sidebars with tips on solo hiking, outdoor etiquette, travel photography, and more. It's a healthy mix of practical how-to and honest first-person narrative, as told to me.

My hope is that the advice and stories in *She Explores* will inspire you to plan that next backpacking trip, on-the-road adventure, or transformative journey: whether it's an artistic, entrepreneurial, or exploratory venture. I hope that by reading about their passions, you'll dive deeper into your own.

AN ODE TO EVERY WOMAN WHO HAS EVER BEEN CALLED OUTDOORSY

You, a natural resource.

You who feels like the best version of herself at sunset when the air is crackling and the dirt's between your toes.

You who, as the sun's rising, promises to be quiet and let the dawn share its secret with the day on its own.

You who, at high noon, have almost-but-not-quite dared the sun to burn your skin, imagining the cracked patina leather it would someday become: signs of a life outside. But you know better than to dare the sun anything.

You who have pulled on crusty socks unceremoniously and brushed off those who notice.

You, who know that all the bruises and scrapes from scrambling and rambling are the best because they remind you of being alive. Someone may even point it out: "How'd ya do that?" And you shrug your shoulders, because you honestly don't know.

You who have shed tears on the trail without really knowing why.

You who look at the mountains and think they must know everything about you, and you who look at the sea and are sure that it doesn't care about you at all.

You who have surprised yourself by falling behind the group, and you who have surprised yourself by charging ahead. The trail is the same, but each time, you're the one who's different.

You who, however gracefully, made it. Sometimes it's ugly, and sometimes you move across the water or rock and have never felt lighter.

You who smiles as someone tries to understand why you have to be barefoot at least some portion of the year, or come in with rosy cheeks and wild hair and dirt clinging in clumps to, well, anywhere it can get. And you who don't really need them to understand anyways.

You who have found your remedy—you lucky girl. It takes some years to know about the cure-all of dried sweat and moon-stains.

You, a natural resource, supplied by nature, and made up of it, too. I am proud of you.

MADISON PERRINS

ENTHUSIASTS

Bravery Can
Be Messy

The very act of achieving ambitious goals—
doing the hard work, working past the failures,
and remaining open to adaptation—
transforms us and builds character.

THRU-HIKING THE PACIFIC CREST TRAIL with no prior hiking experience
was my first big outdoor goal. While I failed to thru-hike the trail in one
season, the process of trying, failing, and going back to complete the remain-
der of the trail in a second season gave me the spark to tackle other ambitious
goals like long-distance biking, thru-hiking the Pacific Northwest Trail, and
completing a half Ironman. When I began delving into the outdoors, it started
as the pursuit of a once-in-a-lifetime adventure, but since then it has evolved
into a full-time way of life. It is where I go to meditate, share experiences, accept
a challenge; to sweat it out, get the blood flowing; to balance my mood, get
re-inspired, grieve, and reflect.

Doing things that scare us—whether physical or mental—is the very
definition of bravery. Growing up, I thought bravery was about being bold

and fearless, but as I've explored the backcountry, I've discovered bravery can be messy. It makes us come face-to-face with our most vulnerable selves, it asks us to sit in discomfort, and it asks us to try, fail, get back up, and stretch ourselves. Embracing fear has greatly affected and enhanced my every experience in the outdoors, and it has urged me to share these experiences and thoughts with others. These lessons I've learned have become even more powerful when translated into a template for everyday living. When I'm afraid to tackle things in my career, relationships, health, and beyond, I am reminded that even with trepidation, I can move forward and slowly but surely take one arduous step at a time. Only then will I be able to look back over the hills and valleys and see how far I've come.

JULIE A. HOTZ

My Injured Brain on Nature

I realized that, when I was removed from my daily overstimulated and fast-paced life, I could continue to recover from my brain injury.

FOR THE FIRST FOUR YEARS I had post-concussion syndrome, I suffered from daily migraines, cloudiness, vertigo, fatigue, depression, and issues with memory and retention. Over time, I learned to identify my triggers and, with the help of a few incredible doctors, developed ways to manage my physical symptoms. More recently, an amazing traumatic brain injury (TBI) community I found through the organization LoveYourBrain has provided me with the emotional support I craved. Today, eight years after my college lacrosse injury, my symptoms no longer present themselves on a daily basis, and I work hard to control them.

The first two years with my injury, I couldn't drive, be in direct sunlight, or look at a computer or television without inducing symptoms, but it was my inability to exercise that I obsessed over. I held on to the hope that I might wake up one morning and feel like my old self again, and my progress was

always tracked against my past sense of balance as a full-time athlete. As time passed, I forgot what that old balance even felt like and, eventually, began to carve out ways to feel comfortable in my new body.

The first shift came during the Adirondack Semester in college: for three months, I lived with eleven other students, no running water, and limited electricity in a secluded yurt village. I realized that, when I was removed from my daily overstimulated and fast-paced life, I could continue to recover from my brain injury.

When I signed up for the National Outdoor Leadership School (NOLS) in Wyoming a few years later, my sole intention was to test this theory. Up to that point, I did not have energy to spare for exercise, and I was hyper-aware that should the course prove too much, my migraines would most likely force me to be evacuated from the Wind River Range. This was terrifying.

But it was time for me to take ownership of my injury.

The last day of my NOLS course was the proudest day of my life. I made it through all four weeks on the course without a single migraine, and I left the strongest and fullest self I had been for more than six years. I know my body and mind better than anyone. The NOLS course reminded me to trust in that knowledge.

But most importantly, I was reminded of what it meant to be in control of my own life. That my brain does do better when I spend more time outdoors and less time behind a screen. When I decide to take the time to step back, reflect, and reassess, my body responds positively. I am a stronger person because of my injury, not just in spite of it.

CAITLIN WARD

In Constant Search of Foliage

Seeking out and engaging with nature
in the urban environment helps me reset my
perspective on a daily basis and reminds me
that there's beauty worth exploring and
protecting right here.

NATURE SEEKERS' FAVORITE DESTINATIONS are usually awe-inspiring, pristine, and remote. These are the places we yearn to explore and strive to protect. The city, on the other hand, is often seen as a place to escape from, the place you leave behind when you want to "get away from it all." But nature exists here, too. We are nature—my family, my neighbors, and the millions of other people of color who, like me, call this place home. *This*—my city, my street, my weed-covered front stoop—is nature, too. Seeking out and engaging with nature in the urban environment helps me reset my perspective on a daily basis and reminds me that there's beauty worth exploring and protecting right here.

Finding nature in the city isn't as hard as you might think. It's not always grand. Sometimes it's small, gritty, spiky, unkempt. Sometimes it's the stubborn bits of clover that push up through cracks in the sidewalk or the patches of prairie that take advantage of every sunny empty lot. Sometimes it's a gorgeous forest preserve a mile from home or the overgrown tomato plants in the community garden down the street. When I started looking for nature in the city, I found it everywhere. And I found it all beautiful.

I've been a gardener my whole life. My mother filled our home with giant, lush indoor plants, was always picking up abandoned bits of greenery, and checking the local nursery for sales. I absorbed my love of plants (and by extension, nature) from her. Plants were my first connection to the earth and remain my strongest link. They are so powerful and so unassuming. Most people don't even think about them, except as backdrop or window dressing. Without plants, though, we wouldn't and couldn't be here. They make so much possible for us and ask for so little in return.

I'm always learning from plants, finding parallels that show me how to connect more deeply to the world around me, and to myself. The plant cuttings in various stages of growth in my house got me thinking. Taking a cutting is the first step in turning one plant into two. The cutting will start small, but with the right care and attention, it'll become its own plant. To relate this to our lives, any small action or idea can grow into something much bigger, something that, with a little encouragement, can flourish. It's up to us to make sure we take healthy cuttings, and harvest the bits of our lives and experiences that can grow their own roots to become something wild, untamed, and uniquely beautiful.

SIMONE MARTIN-NEWBERRY

SOLO HIKING

Hitting the trail by yourself exposes you to many of the same inherent risks you take on when you travel with a partner or group, including injury, dehydration, hypothermia, wildlife, strangers, and getting lost. But there are also built-in benefits: a clear head, undisturbed time to be yourself, and the pride you'll take in finding your own way.

The decision to hike alone is very personal. Some may never venture to hike by themselves: for them, the risks outweigh the benefits. But for those looking to stretch their legs solo, here are some reminders to tuck in your pocket before you head out:

1. Plan your route ahead of time and let someone else know where you're headed—a friend, family member, significant other, or local park ranger. Give them your route and timeline so they know if/when to come looking.

2. Get comfortable with the terrain, pay attention to your physical experience, and figure out a pace that works for you.

3. Trust your instincts. If an incline feels above your skill level, wait to tackle it with a partner on a future trip.

4. Choose a "turnaround" time before you set out. This is the time of day that you will turn around and head back to the trailhead, whether or not you reach your goal for the day. Keep an eye on your watch and the setting sun.

5. Bring a map and compass. Take note of landmarks as you pass them—a digital camera or cell phone can be a great way to time-stamp these bread crumbs.

6. Stay on the trail; it will keep you oriented and protect the natural landscape.

7. Always practice Leave No Trace (for more details on the Leave No Trace philosophy, visit lnt.org.)

8. Pack a basic first aid kit, emergency blanket, knife (or multi-tool), and headlamp. Also take a lighter and fire-starting tinder so you can build a fire for warmth and to signal for help if necessary. Make sure to brief yourself on responsible backcountry fire practices.

9. Wear bright colors and bring extra layers, including a raincoat. Always assume it's going to rain.

10. Carry more water than you think you'll need. At least a liter for every two hours on the trail is a good standard. Bring a small water filter or iodine tablets in case you need to fill up on the trail.

11. Bring lots of snacks!

12. Keep yourself company. Resist the urge to tune into a podcast or listen to music. Whistle a tune. Breathe in the smell of the trees. Marvel at the distance you covered. Bring a notebook to record your thoughts and ideas—you might want to return to this headspace when you get home.

13. And above all, trust in the voice in your head that powers you up the trail.

As We Are

Even on the worst days, especially on the
darkest ones, I know I have to get out
into deep green spaces and find gratitude
for what my body is capable of.

I'VE SPENT A LOT OF MY LIFE trying to keep up with my mom. As a kid I was often perplexed as to how my mom had so much energy. We were always hiking, biking, skiing, camping, and playing outside. To this day my fiercest competition on the ski course is my sixty-three-year-old mother.

I look up to my mom as an example of how to live a full life, regardless of what it throws at you. I was often in awe of the strength and perseverance it took for her to keep going when life knocked her down. My mom was in a car accident and in a coma for weeks, leaving her with a traumatic brain injury. She fought through multiple miscarriages and a divorce. She has suffered broken collarbones and hips and had a mastectomy. Her emotional and physical pain has in no way defined who she is, but has made her stronger.

My "injuries" are a little less obvious. They lurk in my gut and in the shadows and are easily covered up with a big smile or a perfectly timed laugh. They are the demons of irritable bowel syndrome (IBS) and depression.

They come creeping in on the best days and stomp all over me on the worst ones. They whisper lies and shout false truths, and I believe them most of the time.

On a recent kayak camping trip to the Adirondacks with my mother, we discovered that we both come to the outdoors to seek that extra light, sparkle, and love that comes from accepting ourselves as we are. And then, when we return to our structural homes with new scabs healing our scrapes and our hearts, we're a bit stronger. The faint scent of campfire that lingers on our jackets reminds us of the place where we feel whole.

I think that while nature can be a thick salve, the real healing comes with the rest and reflection after the adventure—the moments spent sipping a hot cup of coffee, savoring a hard-earned chocolate chip cookie, or soaking in a hot tub. Even on the worst days, especially on the darkest ones, I know I have to get out into deep green spaces and find gratitude for what my body is capable of. I have to continue to make beautiful memories to replace the bleak thoughts my illnesses make.

If there's one thing I've learned from my mother's tenacity, it's that taking a chance on the outdoors is always worth it.

GRETCHEN POWERS

Running into Something Bigger than Myself

You can set yourself up to succeed by making success your only option.

MY LOVE OF RUNNING and my love of landscapes have evolved together. I've always been creative, and I pursued art in college, but it wasn't until I found long-distance running that the two started to inform each other. My creative thinking really developed out on the trails, and my art projects were greatly influenced and inspired by the landscapes I was running through. It was a beautiful interaction—I would take off from campus on a twenty-mile run and I'd trace the beach, then I'd run through a canyon to a waterfall, and back to the beach to soak in the ocean. Now I am running in the epic and inspiring moutains of the Eastern Sierra, learning these backcountry trails and coming upon the most stunning scenes through my running. I am motivated by the land, and I love the intimacy of learning a landscape on my own two feet.

I'm fascinated by pattern and repetition of lines and the shapes that emerge in landscapes. More often than not the compositions of my photos center around lines of the land, such as patterned snow on a mountain, or puddles and moss in the dirt. I'm intrigued by elements coming together: that middle ground. There's so much energy in that spot where land and seasons shift.

Not only has running helped inspire my creative pursuits, it has also allowed me to dive into something bigger than myself. I'm a two-time Olympic athlete, and one of Saudi Arabia's first ever female athletes. It was the most unexpected thing: I got an invitation from the International Olympic Committee to compete a month and a half before the opening ceremony of the 2012 London Olympics. This was this first time that Saudi Arabia sent female athletes, and the first Olympics where every country had female representation. I'm so grateful that I had that opportunity. It was one of those times where you lean into the unexpected. Running in the Olympic Games and being part of a historical event helped me find my speaking voice and passion for storytelling.

My participation was a pretty groundbreaking moment. I was doing so many interviews and in that situation there is no other option than to be on top of it. It was so important to properly convey the message and my story. That's one of the most powerful lessons: you can set yourself up to succeed by making success your only option. This can be translated into so many other areas of life. I also learned the importance of telling your own story. Only you have the ability to speak to it genuinely. I figured if I was going to be in the news, the information might as well come directly from the source. There was definitely pressure being in that position, being a top news story, but with that pressure I was called to rise to the occasion, to be genuine and positive.

Now I'm training to qualify for the Tokyo 2020 Olympics in the marathon. On a personal level, it's a daunting and inspiring goal. It will be the first time that any woman qualifies for Saudi Arabia. How meaningful to show that not only are we participating and able, we are here and qualified.

SARAH ATTAR

For the Love of Climbing

Every worthwhile experience starts small,
with a dream, but can be attained with
perseverance and sheer curiosity.

SINCE I SWUNG MY FIRST PAIR OF ICE TOOLS when I was twenty-four,
I've been incapable of imagining a life without climbing. My twenties were an
amorphous time, and by letting passion hold the reins, I allowed climbing to
shape every facet of my life. When I was twenty-seven, I quit my job, packed
what possessions I could fit in my car, and left New York City to live on the
road indefinitely.

I spent twelve months immersed in the climbing "dirtbag" lifestyle, buoyed
by the belief that the satisfying things in life were still free—companionship,
love, and laughter. I traveled to Africa on a big-wall expedition and, one year
later, aid-soloed my first big wall in Zion National Park. Climbing was about
discovering the difference between impossible and possible, and where I lay
on that spectrum. It was about learning how to restructure my life, from the
ground up. It was about understanding that every worthwhile experience starts
small, with a dream, but can be attained with perseverance and sheer curiosity.

Climbing taught me to accept responsibility for myself; if I was competent enough to learn the technical skills, I could also be confident enough to play the primary role.

Our lives don't follow a predefined arc, but we can create our own personal history through writing. Doing so taught me not to deliberately conceal certain feelings, such as fear of failure, and that choosing vulnerability is an act of courage vital to storytelling.

When we show up as we really are, whether we mean to or not, we create a community built on trust, empathy, and authenticity. It's scary to admit that you don't have it all figured out, but sharing the complicated and imperfect parts of our lives builds bridges instead of walls. It sends a message to everyone around us that life is made up of highs and lows, rather than just a highlight reel of best moments. Writing creates a space for others to feel safe enough to share their stories, and it is an indescribably powerful feeling to discover that other people relate to your struggle.

As much as I have been afraid of being vulnerable, I craved it at the same time. Just like a bold climb, part of the scariness is beautiful. The intimidating aspect of a rock climb is not always falling and injuring yourself, but the transparency of the ordeal. Much like in life, we put it all out there in order to reach the summit, telling the world: "This is me! This is who I am, here is a shortcoming, please don't judge me. Please accept me."

KATHY KARLO

CREATIVES

I Am an Artist

I think of art as magic; I can bring
something to life that doesn't exist yet.

I GREW UP ON THE SEA; my mom worked on ships and homeschooled
me, and we traveled for most of my childhood, hopping between boats, a
small farm, and everywhere from Texas, to New York, to Pennsylvania. My
self-identity grew from a restless mixture of air and water instead of roots. I
found who I was in movement and imagination and solitude and wild places,
a combination that has both served and challenged me. Now I see that this
is where my artwork stems from—discovering who I am, and who I want to
be, as a woman in the wild. I hope everyone who connects with my art can be
moved by that wild woman in some way, as I often am, as she reminds me to
create boldly, explore bravely, and live fiercely.

There was no single "moment" that caused me to suddenly identify as
an artist. Truthfully, there are times when I *still* don't feel like one. I had to
force-feed myself the idea. The statement "I am an artist" starts as a whisper, a
half-truth you mutter under your breath, glancing out of the corners of your
eyes, hoping no one finds out you're a fraud. This identity grows slowly, often
painfully, until one day when a stranger asks you, "What do you do?" you say,
"I am an artist." You feel proud. You *are* an artist! And then you go home and
overanalyze those words for the next week.

I think of art as magic; I can bring something to life that doesn't exist yet. Isn't that wild? It doesn't just involve putting a brush or pen to paper. It's also this full, sometimes-messy experience of gathering inspiration and ideas, letting them brew in my mind for a while, and then one day, somehow, letting all that spill into a singular idea, painting, collage, drawing.

I am pulled to representing the female form because I like to think every woman I draw is in some way me, or a future me—strong, independent, resourceful, in-the-moment, brave—and hope women viewers will see themselves in the works as well.

AMANDA SANDLIN

The Musical Mountaineers

Many people ask us when we are going to perform, but part of the true magic of what we are doing is coming across our summit concerts unexpectedly.

EVER SINCE MY GRANDPA gave me my first keyboard, it's been a lifelong dream of mine to play piano on a mountain summit. The climbing class required me to train with a forty-five-pound pack, the same weight of my backcountry keyboard backpack. There is something personally satisfying about carrying my piano in a sixty-liter backpack to fulfill a lifelong dream of creating music on a mountain summit. —Rose

AS A KID, I was severely bullied and I struggled to find my place in the world. I started playing violin when I was four and spent most of my time outside exploring and hiking. Music and the mountains have always been my refuge— they are the two things in my life that allow me to be exactly who I am, without judgment. —Anastasia

We are both mountain climbers and lifelong musicians. Through a curious sequence of events, we were brought together and discovered a shared dream of carrying our instruments, the violin and piano, into the wilderness to perform. Our original audience included Mount Pilchuck, Monte Cristo, Sloan Peak, Mount Baker, and the rest of the Cascade Range. On the audio for our very first concert, we can be heard saying, "I wonder if anybody heard us?"

Finding the Musical Mountaineers in the wilderness is akin to spotting a Sasquatch—we don't announce our concerts and we are usually up and down the mountain before most people are even arriving at the trailhead. Many people ask us when we are going to perform, but part of the true magic of what we are doing is coming across our summit concerts unexpectedly. We are also very aware of Leave No Trace ethics, and we are very conscientious about not having oversized groups in the wilderness.

On the day of a backcountry concert, we typically wake up at a ridiculously early hour—sometimes as early as 1 or 2 a.m. We drive to the trailhead, often feeling so excited that we are jittery and almost buoyant with energy. The hike begins in the dark, by the light of the moon and our headlamps. As the sun starts to rise, anticipation of the concert increases: "Will we make it to the summit before sunrise? Will we be too cold? Will the wind die down?" Every Musical Mountaineers adventure has its own challenges. Strings go out of tune quickly in the cool, thin air. Blustery winds send sheet music down the mountainside like paper airplanes. The buildup is intensely exciting—we frantically put on dresses, set up camera equipment, and retrieve our instruments. Despite our concerns, when our notes first drift into the crisp mountain air, everything is perfect.

The music and the mountains are two powerfully emotional languages that speak to every single person. Our dream is to use this powerful combination to remind people of all the good in the world.

ROSE FREEMAN AND ANASTASIA M. ALLISON

Time to Recharge

I'm not motivated by things that come easily. The reward at the end of a struggle is what drives me forward. That's why I love climbing mountains.

EVEN AS SOMEONE WHO LOVES HER JOB, I often feel the need to escape. Going outside offers me some perspective and a much-needed break from my creative business. Because I both live and work out of my house, I sometimes feel like I'm always working. That's why weekends in the mountains are so important for me. It gives me time to step away from the e-mails and truly refocus on what's important, which, for me, is making new memories with friends (or my dog) in nature.

I'm not motivated by things that come easily. The reward at the end of a struggle is what drives me forward. That's why I love climbing mountains. If you'd asked me ten years ago if I'd ever climb Mount Rainier, I would have laughed and said, "*No way.*" That's what's exciting—doing what I would have considered crazy before. I've learned not to say "I'll never do that," because so often I've proved myself wrong.

You need persistence to make a living as an artist. There will be countless obstacles, letdowns, and failures. I'm constantly trying to figure out how to stay relevant, how to market my business effectively. But there will also be victories, and that's what you have to hold tight while you let the other, not-so-great things go. Keep finding enjoyment in art and give yourself time to step away when necessary. Whatever you do, keep that goal laser-focused, and don't give up on yourself.

BROOKE WEEBER

HOW TO STAY CREATIVELY INSPIRED

Our creative endeavors take many shapes: pen-and-ink drawings, needlepoint, plein air watercolors, the perfect granola bar, poetry. And whether or not your ambition is also your livelihood, enthusiasm and creativity wane now and again.

Here are some tips for how exploration can help you regain your creative inspiration:

STEP OUTSIDE Fresh air does wonders for the restless mind. No need to devote the whole day (but by all means if you can spare it!)—an hour's walk through a city park or a short hike on a local trail is the perfect reset.

SWITCH MEDIUMS If you've been staring at a computer monitor all week, change to analog. Using your hands to knead bread or knit a scarf or build a fire will make room for growth. It can also help you think through a problem: a pen and paper can take down whatever block the computer screen had thrown up.

START FROM SCRATCH If you feel like you're treading the same path over and over again, it's okay to scrap a well-worn mindset and begin once more. Often, inspiration and confidence are found in starting again.

LEARN SOMETHING NEW Prepare to feel humbled but inspired by the challenge of gaining knowledge and skill.

HANG OUT WITH KIDS The younger, the better. You may notice kids have a certain confidence, are proud of what they make, and don't limit their ideas or stories the way adults sometimes do. Their youthful perspectives are contagious.

GO EASY ON YOURSELF It's okay to not always be creating. It's okay to un-curate your life.

VISIT A MUSEUM Even if you're not a visual artist, there's a comfort in being surrounded by color. Exposure to others' work and history in a low-pressure environment coaxes new thought.

TALK TO SOMEONE DIFFERENT Seek out someone you respect from a completely different discipline, medium, market, or job. Ask what they're working on, what's got them stuck, or what's inspiring them. Help them. Applying your mind to a new challenge can free you up in your own work.

SLEEP UNDER THE STARS Disconnecting for a full twenty-four hours is especially generative. After setting up camp and cooking a simple meal, all that's left to do is relax with your thoughts and the night air.

Dropping a Line

Art was a way for me to have control,
to create beauty from within.

MY RELATIONSHIP WITH THE OUTDOORS began in high school, when my friends and I would go hiking to spend time together away from our parents. The summer after I graduated high school, I went on my first backpacking trip for sixteen days in the North Cascades, and I was hooked. Then I started climbing in the gym when I started college. Climbing was my gateway sport. Biking and skiing followed seamlessly. I've been addicted to the adrenaline ever since.

I started doing my line art when I was eighteen. I didn't think I was very beautiful or cool, and I was new to outdoor sports. I wanted to be like the gorgeous and talented athletes and artists that popped up on my social media feed. Art was a way for me to have control, to create beauty from within.

I spend a lot of time making it seem as if I'm organized and have my life together, but this isn't my reality. I used to be self-conscious about my lack of focus or sometime laser-beam hyper-focus. I've grown to embrace these aspects of myself. When I create art, I concentrate entirely, as though I'm

working on the most important project in the world. When I ride my bike or ski, I can be my weirdest and not-so-focused self. Ego and id do overlap.

Dropping a line on skis or a bike has intent in the same way that dropping a line on paper has. When I am skiing, climbing, or biking, I seek out ways to make things more stylish and flowing in a similar way to creating art.

BROOKLYN BELL

Lady
Lock Off

Photography started out as a curiosity
and gave way to a voice and a passion that
has enriched my life in so many ways.

"I THOUGHT THERE was no place for me in a world of rugged men clothed in dark earth tones. And then I realized . . . nature makes rainbows, too."

I wrote these words reflecting on my journey into the climbing world. When I read them out loud to a friend, I was surprised when my voice cracked and I started to get teary. I realized just how much they say about who I am today. The climbing community builds itself. Through climbing you have this wonderful common interest and it weaves and interconnects you with complete strangers.

Photography started out as a curiosity and gave way to a voice and a passion that has enriched my life in so many ways. My favorite photos are those that capture joy or strength. One photo of a woman climbing changed my perception of what I could or couldn't do, and I can only hope that my photography does the same.

I like to share what personally inspires me. Most of us are not pushing the limits of climbing, we are pushing the limits of ourselves. It is about capturing that struggle and accomplishment in all of us and not just the elite few.

IRENE YEE

Stepping Out

*Self-doubt and a comfy job
held me back for the longest time.*

I'VE DRAWN LANDSCAPES since I was a teen. I lived in a small town and always wanted to escape, so I drew the places I daydreamt about. Out of habit, I continued to draw from other references, and one day I realized I was limiting myself and my perspective. From there, I made it a point to leave town every year to see someplace new and to find my own references and experiences. Now most of my drawings are from my travels, and each art piece is a part of me and who I am.

I was my own biggest obstacle to becoming a full-time artist. Self-doubt and a comfy job held me back for the longest time. It's hard to take a chance, especially when there are no art clients on the horizon. I had to trust that my self-motivation, passion, and hard work would get me where I want to be. Being an artist is learning to deal with rejection and doubt. It's difficult for artists because our work is both personal and professional. Rejection hurts more because you pour your heart into your work. Doubt builds when no one reaches out, but we learn most about ourselves from these moments and we train to push forward.

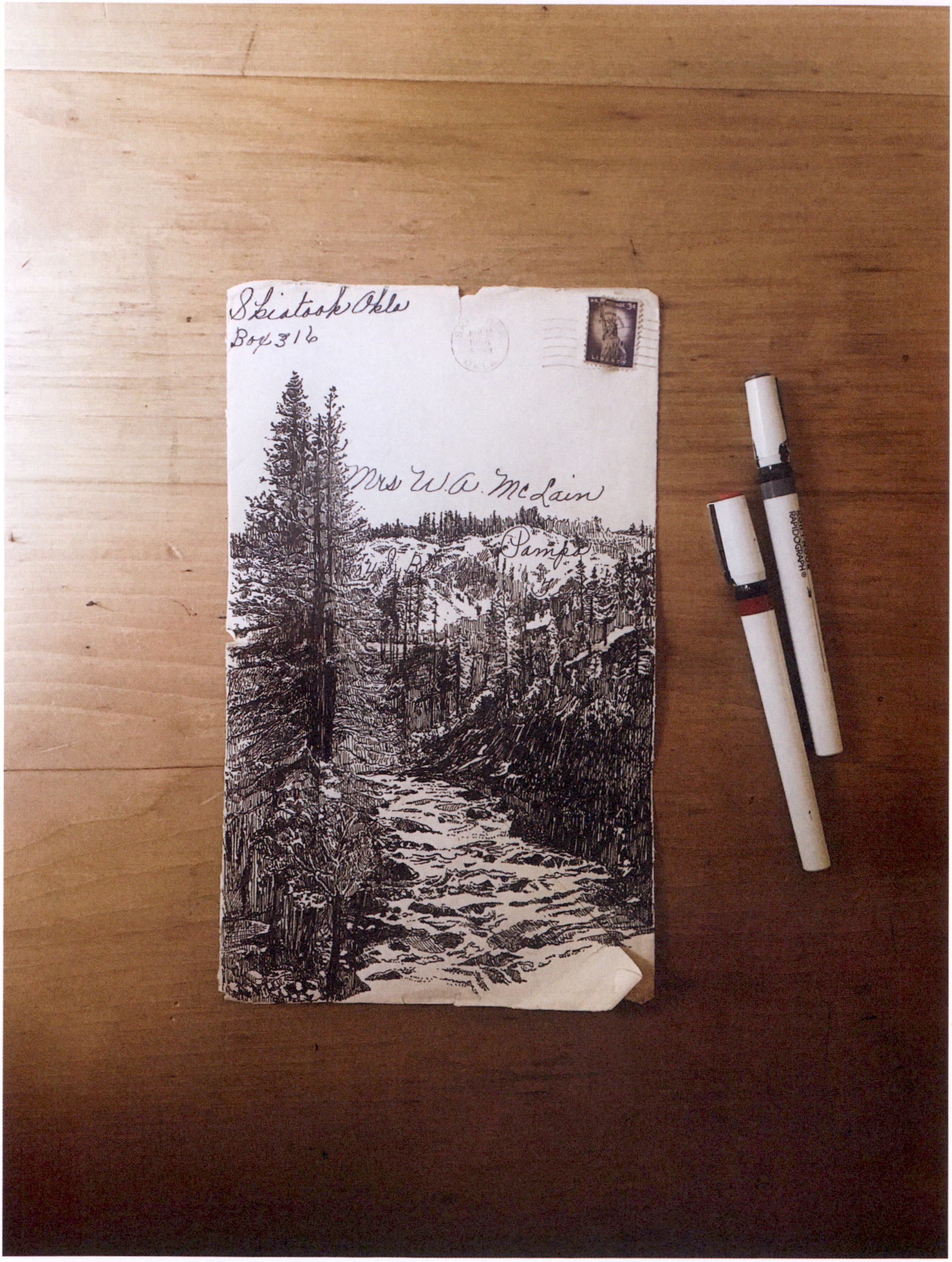
Skiatook Okla
Box 316
Mrs W.A. McLain
Pampa

There are going to be moments in my work where I get lost. I question myself, my motives, and my goals. During these struggles, I have to remain focused and push through, even when it's slow and painful. The world feels so instantaneous that sometimes I lose the sense of how much work goes into creating. The most incredible work must contain passion, madness, relief, and, some days, delusion, but it will never be instantaneous.

SAM LEE

FOUNDERS AND PROFESSIONALS

Founding Eastern Sierra Conservation Corps

Trail work showed me what
I am capable of.

THERE WASN'T ONE MOMENT where I thought, yes, I am going to start Eastern Sierra Conservation Corps. It was a collection of many moments, built on experience and the intention to provide more opportunities for young people to experience wild spaces. I thought, "Why not give it a shot?" If one life could be affected, it would be worth it.

Trail work showed me what I am capable of. It has taken me to sights I never would have seen otherwise. It has introduced me to a family of loving, determined, brilliant, and funny humans, and I wanted to show this world to others. The landscape of the Eastern Sierra is so diverse and dynamic. The tall mountain peaks are wild, raw, and unforgiving. There are dramatically serene alpine lakes and delicate meadows, mixed with weather that can turn on you in a moment's notice. It is no secret, there are not a lot of people who

look like me working in our National Parks and Forests. Women, particularly women of color, are the least represented group in employment in and visitation to public lands. Each women-based trail crew we fund contributes to evening the playing field.

The mountains do not discriminate; they don't care who you are, where you came from, or what your skin color is. They demand your respect.

AGNES VIANZON

Science for Conservation

I remember being nine years old and wondering who was going to save the tiger.

I CAN RECALL WITH VIVID DETAIL lying belly-down, chin on my arms, the hot sun beating down on my scratched-up legs as I watched tadpoles metamorphose into froglets. I spent the summers of my childhood like this, smelling like mud and the lily pads that grew in the creek by my house. As a child, I didn't know people could make a living staring at frogs. Today, I combine my curiosity of the natural world with my overwhelming need to make the world a better place. And sometimes this means I get to stare at frogs all day, or work with carnivore DNA. Everyone answers a particular call. For me, it's using science for wildlife conservation.

Knowledge is liberating. Have you ever studied something just for the sake of learning it? When we learn, we understand, and we want to learn more. I encourage others to be passionate about the outdoors and science because I know I can't do it alone. Wildlife conservation and environmental stewardship need people of all backgrounds and interests in order to secure a sustainable future. I remember being nine years old and wondering who was

going to save the tiger. Hopefully, it'll be me, but it'll also be you, your friend, your mom, your neighbor. We'll do it together.

When you think of scientists, do you automatically think of a white man in a lab coat? I have a lab coat, but I'm not a man, I'm often covered in dirt, and my hair is a tangled mess. And yet I'm a scientist. Scientists have a public image problem, and it's centered on us being seen as cold: warmth, trust, and credibility are traits I think many scientists have to work hard for in order to be given space on a particular platform. As a woman, I have had to work twice as hard to receive less than the same amount of consideration as my male counterparts. We want to spend our time talking about science, not justifying our qualifications or proving that we can hike that mountain.

Professionally, I can't take credit for discovering anything entirely novel and unheard of, but I have experienced a lot of things for the very first time and been utterly fascinated by them. Whether it was the results of my master's degree on bobcat ecology or learning how to catch salamanders for the first time, they were my discoveries, and the whole experience was *awesome*. I want everyone to feel that way. It's empowering, it's invigorating . . . it's living. Whatever it is, you don't have to be a biologist to feel endless wonder with discovering something in nature. Maybe five thousand people have seen that summit view, or swam in that river, or watched a tadpole grow legs, but the feeling of living it, discovering it, is yours.

IMOGENE CANCELLARE

Hiking My Way through Motherhood

On the trail, the bonds I made were tighter than with friends I had had for much of my adulthood.

I LIKE TO SAY THAT I HIKED my son Mason out of me. I was forty-one when I had him, and in the days leading up to his birth, my doctors threatened to induce me because of my advanced maternal age. The day before Mason was born, I hiked three miles, up and down hills, talking to him and asking him to please come out. That night I went into labor. I was tired the week after he was born but quickly became restless. I wanted to be outside with him, not cooped up in a room. So I asked some women I met in a new mama group to join me for a trail walk. The first week, five women met me, and then eleven, and then fourteen, and it only grew from there. Instantly these women became my friends. On the trail, the bonds I made were tighter than with friends I had had for much of my adulthood.

Hike it Baby started with Mason and me but became this incredible, nationwide community around us, a warm cocoon that helped my son and I grow together. I felt strong hiking with a baby. I had always seen myself as a "big girl" and never felt very graceful on the trail. Once I had Mason and Hike it Baby, I found my stride through carrying Mason and leading others. With motherhood I felt a new pride in my strong body, and suddenly my wide hips and jiggling body mattered less.

Nature is the great neutralizer. No matter who you are, your baby will barf or poo on you, your hair will always be a mess, your clothes will never be perfect, you will realize you ran out the door without your kids' shoes or wipes. This is motherhood. In the outdoors, none of that matters. There's never a hike I go on with moms where someone isn't giving another mom an extra jacket, a snack, a lift, a diaper, whatever it is that's needed. The outdoors brings women together and takes away the traditional barriers we build.

Our society needs nature now more than ever. Children benefit when many of their early sensory experiences are out in nature, walking paths, being held by a mother or father or caregiver. Being in the outdoors helps children understand the world better. Through experiencing the natural world, they learn patterns, colors, sound. Everything a child learns in a classroom can start when they're a baby or toddler, crawling on a trail or throwing stones in a creek. Go outside with your baby as soon as you feel comfortable, perhaps first sitting in the park, then venturing onto a trail, moving, hiking, and so on. The benefit to both the parent and the child is noticeable, and these will be the memories your child will have as an adult.

SHANTI HODGES

BUILDING BONDS IN THE OUTDOORS

Adulthood's distractions aren't conducive to making new friends. Piling to-do lists, side hustles, and family commitments are just a few of the many reasons the phrase "too busy" leaves our lips. The best way to fast-track a friendship is to take it outside. Whether you're ambling in your local park or on a multiday backpacking trip, a shared experience away from the constraints of a coffee date provides opportunities for deep, thoughtful conversation and connection.

Here are some ways to meet new people and forge bonds in the outdoors:

ASK If you meet someone you like at a networking event and you want to get to know her better, ask her outside.

GO ONLINE TO GET OFFLINE Using social media, you can find communities for every activity, in many corners of the world. Some are grassroots organizations, others are run through outdoors nonprofits like the Appalachian Mountain Club. The structure of these groups means you can depend on an organizer and interact with attendees before you even step outside.

TAKE A WALK Use your lunch break at work to stroll around the neighborhood. Invite a coworker to join you and challenge yourself not to talk about work.

PLAN A TRIP This is a larger undertaking, but the payoff is worth it (and planning can be equally fun!). Gather a group to hike a bucket-list backpacking trip, raft a river, or soak in a hot spring. You'll be telling the stories for years.

ATTEND AN EVENT Research what's happening in your local area. Check the flyers at your climbing gym or hiking lodge. What excites you? Surround yourself with people who are as enthusiastic as you.

MAKE A STANDING DATE Whatever the activity of choice, affix it to the calendar. Commit the first and third Saturdays of the month to, say, snowshoeing. Invite your friends to put it on their calendars, too. Encourage them to share with others that might be into breaking trail.

GO ANYWAY You never know who you might bump into when you're doing what you love.

DON'T GET DISCOURAGED Finding new friends and deepening those friendships takes time and often goes in fits and starts. That's the reality of adulthood. Don't give up! Keep looking for ways to connect.

On the Fireline

I am who I am because of the experiences
I've had on the fireline.

I AM MOST MYSELF WHEN I'M MOVING. This is true of everything I do, and particularly firefighting. I crave being on the move, seeing new country, and working so hard I can barely remain upright while eating dinner at fire camp. Knowing what it is to slide into a sleeping bag feeling as if there isn't another ounce of exertion in my body has empowered me in ways I can't quite describe—I am who I am because of the experiences I've had on the fireline.

The job is different every day. You can be napping in the truck one minute and be digging "hotline" the next. You work all day on a task, then you go to a camp and eat and sleep, then wake up and do it again, usually for fourteen-day assignments. I appreciate the hard work and long hours, but I particularly enjoy the bonds you create with the people you work with. Even if we get annoyed with each other, there's no better way to make good friends than to spend every waking hour together, traveling, eating, and lying in your sleeping bag next to them.

I recommend firefighting to anyone who has entertained even the briefest thought of doing it. Whether you think you're not "tough" enough, if you have the true desire to work hard and can put aside the comforts you're used to, you'll find that you have a lot more grit than you thought.

AMANDA MONTHEI

Using Archaeology to Speak for History

I feel a sense of duty to protect the Ojibwe land my ancestors managed for centuries before me. My mentors tell me to think ahead to the next seven generations because the earth is borrowed from them.

NATIVE AMERICAN ARCHAEOLOGISTS empower Indigenous people by giving us a voice in deciding how our cultural resources are managed and how our histories are interpreted. An Ojibwe woman, I entered the field to help meet the need for more Indigenous archaeologists. Finding artifacts is exciting. This summer I uncovered a projectile point that had not been held by another human for five thousand years. The thrill of holding artifacts my ancient Indigenous ancestors expertly crafted or sitting next to the same hearth my forebears sat beside a millennia before inspires me.

Whenever I travel, I bring my running shoes. It is an efficient and potent way to experience new environments: temperature, elevation, ground, light, and surroundings are things runners must pay attention to.

Hiking or walking with a camera in hand allows me to experience land in similar ways to running, but more creatively. Shooting photos is meditative. For that short moment when I am setting up to take the picture, I am completely absorbed. Holding my breath, stabilizing my hand, and timing the shutter release brings a concentration that is often hard to find in my scatter-brained mind.

Photography is what inspired me to become a climber. I dreamt of reaching the rocky, awe-inspiring vistas I saw in climbing photographs. A semester into my PhD program in Tucson, I started climbing.

Acknowledging whose land I am recreating on reminds me, and whoever listens to me, that we are on Indian land. Because I am on Indian land, I say *miigwech* ("thanks") to the land and the ancestors who managed the land for centuries before me by praying and giving tobacco as an offering. I recognize Indigenous histories that many of us were not taught in school. Before European colonization, millions of Native Americans thrived on Turtle Island—a.k.a. North America. Today, more than five hundred tribal nations are recognized by the United States. All these tribes have ties to the land we live and recreate on, whether those lands are urban centers or remote, natural spaces.

Although the land looks "wild" and untouched by humans, it's not. Indigenous people have been swindled out of much of the land treaties were supposed to reserve for them, but we have lived here since time immemorial. Traveling around North America, it is easy to find ancient objects lying on the ground. Pottery sherds, projectile points, and stone tools are everywhere if you look closely enough.

Native America has also left behind monumental architecture. Huge irrigation canals, giant medicine wheels, enormous earthen mounds, intricate rock dwellings, and more dot Turtle Island.

I feel a sense of duty to protect the land my ancestors managed for millennia before me. My mentors tell me to think ahead to the next seven generations because the earth is borrowed from them. This worldview cultivates actions based on sustainability and reciprocity. Reciprocal relationships in which we care for everything around us, including animals, water, rocks, plants, landforms, and the cosmos, are vital to keeping the earth healthy for future generations.

ASHLEIGH THOMPSON

TAKING YOUR CAREER OUTSIDE

The outdoor industry bleeds into other sectors like tourism, retail, manufacturing, and entertainment, not to mention public service. There truly are a lot of ways to take your career outside. Whether you're looking to stay local, open to anywhere in your country, or hoping to see the world, there's a great fit waiting for you.

Here are some avenues to explore:

PUBLIC SERVICE The National Park Service, the US Forest Service, AmeriCorps, Conservation Corps, and even the Peace Corps all provide opportunities to work in public service and spend substantial time outside in the preservation of natural beauty around the country and the world.

OUTDOOR PROGRAMS If you love to teach and lead, outings-based employment might be the right track for you. Guiding companies like National Outdoor Leadership School (NOLS), REI, Outward Bound, and Appalachian Mountain Club all run outdoor programming and need certified guides to lead them.

BRANDS If you have a corporate skillset, bringing it to an outdoor brand is often the easiest transition into the outdoor industry. Making the switch to an outdoor brand gets you close to the vision for an activity or market as well as the lifestyle.

MEDIA Traditional publications offer opportunities with dependable reputations, and the explosion of independent digital publishing has led to even more freelance options.

HOSPITALITY No matter where people go to recreate, they need a place to stay. Explore who's doing sustainable hospitality in your area of choice. Certain positions even offer housing in remote areas.

SCIENCE We're still only scratching the surface of how our endlessly intertwined and interdependent planet functions. But, with each layer we peel back, the better suited we are to intelligently conserve it and take sustainable action.

VOLUNTEERING You don't have to make your living in the outdoor industry to be a part of it and make a difference. Seeking out volunteer opportunities can be a great way to get out, learn new skills, make new friends (with similar interests), and even travel. Keep on the lookout for job postings and open calls for a foot in the door.

ENTREPRENEURSHIP Starting your own business is another way into the outdoor industry. Don't dismiss your idea for a better piece of gear or guiding service for your favorite single-track route. Voids in the market always exist; listen for their potential.

Here and Farther

*Over time I have settled into the idea
of there being power in delicacy.*

PLEIN AIR PAINTING was the reason I started my career as a National Park
ranger. I have been able to live and paint in amazing landscapes, and also help
protect them. I have discovered purpose in being a source for artists looking
to participate in National Park residencies.

My style comes from the in-the-moment choices I make when working
outdoors. The pace is set by how long the light on my subject may last, affect-
ing my color choices and brush strokes. My paintings are small, packable. I
can reflect on the composition in real time, physically moving until I find the
painting. Many times I see a great view, hike down the trail a ways in hopes
of something "better," then go back to the first view. Most of the time when I
pass up that initial recognition, I end up hustling back.

I have never not had the will to paint, but I do look to other artists to
refresh my ideas. When I am seeking inspiration from others, I tend toward
books and old textbooks. In college I studied Dutch landscape painting and
can always revisit those expansive views to study how those masters created
depth. The amazing Lois Dodd (still painting at ninety!) is my contempo-
rary influence.

When I shared some work with one of my art school professors a couple of years ago, he called my post-graduation paintings "powerfully delicate." He said it had to do with my mark making and the physical scale of my paintings (small), which surprised me, given my penchant for mountains and wide-angle views. Over time I have settled into the idea of there being power in delicacy. So much of media calls for being louder and bigger, it took time for me to recognize the boldness in a painting that is intimately scaled. A lot of my purpose as a painter is to take home something of the places and times I am living. Pulling painting and sketches from between the leafs of my journal to revisit does bring with it a feeling of tenderness.

MARYELLEN HACKETT

Becoming a Full-Time Mountain Nomad

Creating your path becomes easy once you align with the authentic version of yourself, even when the path you take is unconventional.

I GREW UP IN MANILA and moved with my family to America at the age of thirteen. As a child, my parents didn't have the money nor the time to take us on regular trips, including the mountain areas near the city. It would have been a hardship for my parents to do so with four kids.

In the fifteen years I practiced law, I was living a dual life where I devoted all my free time to planning trips and traveling with others, all of which involved the mountains. My hobby proved to be a calling. I didn't actively search for this path. Guiding treks around the world was never planned. The epiphany happened during a year I was away from my law practice, doing extensive solo treks. As I started to enjoy my own company and silence, my

truest desires ultimately revealed themselves. The answers to the questions we have about our lives reside within us. To reach those answers, you have to be willing to spend time alone. The act of "doing" isn't necessarily what gets us where we need to be.

I returned to my lawyer role with a new set of life philosophies that slowly paved the way for me to overcome my fears. At that point, I knew I'd fallen in love with the nomadic lifestyle and the mountains. I had no choice but to go back to them. The experience changed me completely—from selling all my possessions including my house in the city, to starting Peak Explorations, which is dedicated to sharing with others the joy I experience from trekking mountains. During this period my mother passed away suddenly. Her passing left me with two gifts—clarity and courage. That was when I knew it was time for me to leave the legal profession, become a mountain nomad, and live the vision that I've had for years.

Peak Explorations has taken me to various mountain regions worldwide—the Himalayas, Andes, Albanian Alps, Drakensberg, Mount Roraima, Cordillera Blanca, Kilimanjaro, Patagonia, and more. Our goal is to introduce hikers to lesser-known mountain trails that yield a world-class travel experience. We also support sustainable economic income in remote mountain regions by providing employment opportunities for marginalized groups and women.

Let your voice be the ultimate guide in the decisions you make. Creating your path becomes easy once you align with the authentic version of yourself, even when the path you take is unconventional, or one that you take later in life (I was forty-one when I made the change!). And yes, there will be fears along the way, but trust that they will dissipate as long as you focus on your desires. Soon enough you learn that fear is merely an illusion, whereas your desire is what's real. Always be of service to others—only then will your every move be right.

MARINEL MALVAR DE JESUS

NOMADS

The Simplest Tools

Everything is harder, so it makes
it all more precious.

WE WERE LIVING IN FRANCE in an apartment. My boyfriend, Simon, and I both worked in restaurants. Simon was miserable and I was even more miserable. We had tough bosses and we worked so hard. The status of chefs in France . . . it's not about being creative. It's very military—you need to be obedient. We were out of creativity and out of energy. Simon always wanted to travel and I needed a change. Simon asked, and I said, "Let's do it."

The van is my home. We built it from scratch. Every scrape, every detail has a history and a fun story. I've had many apartments, but this one is a live creature. He's a character. He's a person. He's a pain in the ass.

You have to adapt. You have to change everything you thought you knew before. Everything is harder, so it makes it all more precious. Say, to have a shower—it's not a daily thing. To cook a meal, it takes more time and more energy. I think it's what I like the most.

My chef job was more physically intense than van life, but there's more psychological exhaustion to living in a van and traveling full-time with someone. In the beginning, we felt as if we had to move fast so we could see more every day. It's taken a while to find the right rhythm. It's still something we struggle with. We've done one month per country, but we have twenty-eight countries still to see.

We camp on public and private land—wherever there is no one. Once we find a camp spot, the rest is about food. It's our principal hobby. When we were in commercial kitchens and cooking school, it was all about perfection and fancy recipes. But due to bad experiences in restaurants, I wanted to stop cooking. Van life was all about simplifying. In the end, because we had time and we were more relaxed, we started to embrace being creative again. We started to eat simply. We love spices. We became vegetarians without knowing it.

Our basics are flour, eggs, sugar, vinegar, and salt. We always have these things. They are inexpensive and can be found everywhere. Otherwise, fresh veggies and oil. Pasta, bread, pancakes . . . they are simple but you can make so many things with them.

To bake bread we put a tiny pot in a bigger pot. You put a bit of steam in the big pot. You cook the bread in the tiny pot. The heat flows in the gap between the two. It works so well. It looks like a cake but tastes like a French baguette.

In the van, it is best to have the simplest tools. I like that there are limits, but it's up to my mind to figure it out. Maybe one day I may find the limit and be bored, but not today.

CÉCILE BERTRAND

BEFORE YOU GO

Your wandering is your own—be it for a weekend, a year, or the foreseeable future yawning into the horizon. The following questions will help you form a sense of where you've been, where you're going, and how to get there with intention.

WHAT ROAD HAS BROUGHT YOU HERE? Why do you want to travel? Perhaps you have a pent-up curiosity, or a long-ago road trip planted the seed. Take the time to reflect on where you are in your life and why you're in need of motion.

WHERE DO YOU WANT TO GO? This is the stuff of dreams. The allure of mobile travel is the flexibility of choice. You could likely explore every corner of your country and have appetite for more. Or you could also invest in a plane ticket to New Zealand, fly thousands of miles, and purchase a minivan upon arrival. The beauty is that it's up to you.

WHO INSPIRES YOU? The people who have gone before us shape our travels. There are hundreds of storytellers out there sharing their routes, vehicles, and methods. Use their stories as your launchpad. You'll find a generous handful within these pages.

HOW LONG WILL YOUR TRIP BE? The answer may be a combination of how much time you have and how much time you want. There are so many factors to dictate the length of your travels: Will you be hitting a pause button on your career? Are you building a new life in motion? Do you fantasize about better weekends spent in the outdoors?

HOW MUCH PHYSICAL LIVING SPACE DO YOU NEED? HOW MUCH DO YOU WANT? Our circles are constantly widening and contracting. Think about your sleep and living space, who will fill it, and what mobile home may accommodate it.

WHAT ARE YOU PASSIONATE ABOUT? It is perhaps too simple to ask what brings you joy. Passion is a more complex feeling: it's a driver. If you're carving space in your life, fill it with what moves you forward.

WHO WILL YOU TAKE WITH YOU? Not every excursion is a solo adventure. If you're planning with a partner or a family, ask them these questions, too. And if you have a dog, cat, or other pet, they may guide you as well.

WHAT FEELS LIKE HOME? Home follows you everywhere; some might say it's within you. Consider whether that's a comfort. When you're packing and planning, gather up home and inject it into your possessions and practices.

WILL THE ROAD BRING YOU BACK HERE? There are two sides to this coin. Will you return, physically, to the origin of your travels? Or are you in search of some new place? And while we're constantly growing and changing, is there a chance wandering will take you back to the same place, psychically, that you are now? What does it take to move forward?

WHAT IS STOPPING YOU? Here you are. If your nature has taken you right up to the invisible line between contemplation and decision, what keeps your toes on the line? Imagine what might happen if you stepped over.

Navigating
the Unknown

I love making plans but it's really fun
to throw them out the window.

I'M STILL TRYING to figure out the reasons I'm on this trip.

I have what I call my "trip encyclopedia": I planned day by day what my dream trip would look like. It has driving destinations, the parks or places where I want to be on a certain day, and a list of potential hikes. I starred the ones I really want to do and I made notes like, "This one's really busy" or "This one has gorgeous alpine lakes." I planned ahead for where I could stay overnight. Most days have two or three options. I didn't map out the *whole* trip, because I ran out of time.

I've realized that anything could happen: what if I hit a big heat wave in the desert? I'm starting to go with the flow. I love making plans but it's really fun to throw them out the window.

I'm nervous about the end of this trip. I think about it almost every day. I love being able to pick up and go when I feel like it. I thought that being on the road would bring me some clarity, but that's a lot of expectation to put on a trip. Two and a half months sounds like a lot of time, but maybe it's not enough.

ELLYSA EVANS

Death Dialogue

A lot of people have things left unsaid that
they want to tell people who have died.

I THINK IT CAN BE EASY to look at my story and see the straightforward parts of it: my mom died, and now I live in a van and talk about death and dying. But that's not complete.

There have been many years of sadness and figuring out what I'm doing and why. When you're twenty-two, you don't think that your mom can die. I was thrown into this world of figuring out what my life was going to be like. I chose the route of travel for many reasons, but it started when I told my therapist, "I just want to pick up and leave." And he said "What do you have to lose?"

That's a very sad and liberating thought.

Now, whenever I'm at a crossroads in my life, I ask myself that question.

That first van trip from California to Texas and back to Colorado was messy. I cried so many times. I didn't know what I was doing and I missed my mom. But there's something about being on the road that feels very important to me. It's making this circle. My mom was killed by a truck driver while she was driving. For a long time, I was afraid of driving. I realized that at any moment, I could die on the road. After she died, I couldn't even go down the street to the coffee shop because I was so nervous. When I started driving in my van, I was able to reclaim that experience.

I have an audio recorder that I took on my most recent trip around the country. Whenever I got into conversations with people I met that touched on death and dying, I asked if I could record them. That got me thinking about other ways to capture those conversations that may be unfinished. A lot of people have things left unsaid that they want to tell people who have died. I wanted to make that connection for people. I believe we can normalize the topic of death and dying. From that trip came the idea of a phone booth. I built a mobile phone booth that invites people to pick up the phone and talk to someone who has died.

Now I'm on tour, capturing these conversations, talking about death and dying, and reclaiming that space on the road. I don't have to be afraid of it.

MORGAN BROWN

Long Weekends or Longer Weekends

My hobby is finding new places.
I see so much potential in a map.

BEING OUTSIDE HAS BEEN breathed into me since I was a baby.

When my parents got married, they moved to an old Forest Service cabin in the redwoods near Santa Cruz, California. They were heating the house with wood stoves and making thirty-minute treks into town. They've been that way my whole life.

My parents would roll out a map at the end of every school year and we'd all come to an agreement. They never said, "We're going here." And it never got tiring, because we were allowed to choose where we went. It wasn't vacation; it was life. We camped every other weekend. Twenty minutes from home, forty-five minutes from home. We just camped. I didn't think camping was special, I just thought it was what you did. It inspired a way of life for me.

Now when the map is rolled out in front of me and my husband, Jonnie, I take the lead. My hobby is finding new places. I see so much potential in a map. I'll spend hours poring over books and satellite images and maps. It's fun to imagine yourself in all these places and make plans that you might not even do. Then I remember that I'm in the city and I need to go to work tomorrow, but it's a fun escape, like reading a book.

We always take long weekends or longer weekends. We've yet to take Monday through Friday off work because we both love our jobs.

Jonnie is a minister at a homeless shelter and I'm a development officer at a youth shelter. We miss work when we're not there because we get to serve people that we capital-*L* Love. I serve eighty young people. You don't often get to work for people who inspire you so. You can't have a bad day because there are so many little miracles. I love being able to use my voice to rally support for young people. I hope they someday sit with themselves and say, "I do deserve everything you believe I deserve and more." None of these kids who walk into this building think they are as beautiful as they are.

The fact that the kids I work with haven't seen our local parks is a shame. I'm first-generation American and I was talking with another first-generation American about how our relatives don't always think these public parks are for them. It upsets me but it inspires me to tell my story. I grew up with a giant Mexican family that loves going outside. I hope we can get to a place where our trails and our granite walls are speckled with more people of color than they are now and that there isn't a cultural barrier. I keep this hope in mind when I'm carving out my narrative in the outdoors. I'm learning to spill my guts louder about these important things.

NOËL RUSSELL

SLEEP SPOTS

The world is full of potential sleep spots. In a camper van and even a trailer, you can pull the curtains closed, darken the lights, and rest your head. Here are some tips about picking a spot to sleep while you're on the road:

CAMPING FOR FREE In the United States, the two easiest paths to free camping (or almost-free camping) are public land and city streets. Let's start with the former.

In the United States, the public lands are National Forests and Bureau of Land Management (BLM) land. Scan a map to find the public lands closest to your route. There, unless otherwise posted, you can disperse camp (outside of designated campgrounds) for up to fourteen days. Remember to stay equipped with food and water, and be prepared to go the bathroom in the outdoors, as there are no amenities. Always follow "Leave No Trace" principles when it comes to cooking, camping, and waste, and when you can, leave the landscape you love better than you found it.

Stealth camping on city streets isn't for everyone or every vehicle, and it may take some getting used to. It's as simple as it sounds: find a level spot to park. Consider your surroundings for noise and safety and parking regulations. Make sure your vehicle is as inconspicuous as possible: now is not the time to pop the top of your Westfalia or open the side door to fire up the camp stove. The beauty of road travel is that, more often than not, your home fits into a parking spot, camouflaged beneath streetlights. Cut a low profile and enjoy the cheapest room in the city.

STATE AND PRIVATE CAMPGROUNDS If you're open to more expensive options, organized campgrounds typically offer amenities like showers, toilets, running water, and utility hookups. Depending on your sleep setup and need for amenities, spending money on campgrounds (anywhere from $5 to $40 a night with no hookup) can be the right investment for the evening.

PRIVATE DRIVEWAYS Reconnecting with cousins and far-off friends is a fringe benefit of roaming. If they offer you a couch, take them up on their driveway.

STRANGERS Locals have great recommendations for stealth and inexpensive camping, or they may even open their driveway up to you. It's a great way to meet people and learn more about a local community, but always use your best judgment.

DEPARTMENT STORES Some behemoth retail stores let trailers, vans, and other mobile campers sleep in their parking lots and use their facilities, but make sure to check with the manager that sleeping is actually allowed. If the parking area is not owned by the store, then it may not be.

BACKCOUNTRY If you have the equipment, road trips are the perfect opportunity to make time for backpacking. Even though it's home, living in a vehicle can get cramped. The freedom of setting up camp off a trail is amplified by the fresh air and stars overhead.

SPLURGE Every now and then, a night out of your vehicle in a room with a door can be a healthy reset. Indulging in a hotel or a nice bed-and-breakfast can reinvigorate your curious nature.

Inspiring Others to Try

---

*You can't hold on to much in the van,
but I have this jar full of memories.*

I'VE BEEN OUT OF THE NAVY FOR A YEAR. My husband, Lovell, and I were living in Los Angeles, but it was so expensive. We decided to build out and live in the van Lovell was leasing for work.

I didn't know there were other people who did this, but my husband told me there was a whole community. We noticed there weren't many black people doing it, so we wanted to share our life through our YouTube channel, "Novel Kulture."

I gave myself three months. I thought, if I can do three months, I can do six. If I can do six, I can do nine. We're planning to live this way for two years.

You can't hold on to much in the van, but I have this jar full of memories. When something good happens, I write it down on a slip of paper and put it in the jar. At the end of the year, I'll take them all out and read them.

PARIS LEE

Raising a
Happy Child

I would tell a new mom to just travel.
It's easier than you think.

WHEN I WAS PREGNANT, I thought we'd need so much. You convince yourself you need a stroller and all these toys and all these clothes. Then you get
into this trap where you can't leave the house without pounds of luggage for
the baby. People look at us and think we're accomplishing a big feat, but we
just bring Wilder with us. He's a baby. He doesn't have a feeling that he needs
to consume. He's happy with what's around him. There's less risk taking, but
for the most part, our plans haven't really changed.

With a baby and three dogs, a smaller vehicle wasn't going to work for us.
My husband wanted to be able to go anywhere—over streams, up mountains.
We found the M1079 on eBay and decided to take a chance and buy it; the
rest of life would fall into place. We're slowly building it into a livable space.
Our goal is to live full-time in South America in a year. We want Wilder to
experience life outside of the United States.

With Wilder, we have to travel slower than we would otherwise. There's
only so long he can stay in his car seat. He's pretty good about everything else.

He doesn't get overstimulated. I think because he's been exposed to so many different stimuli on hikes and camping, he doesn't react negatively to new feelings. I love that—it's cool to watch him experience new things.

I would tell a new mom to just travel. It's easier than you think. Your child will adapt. Pushing a little past everyone's comfort zone is important.

Our main goal is to raise a happy child. Perhaps as a teenager he'll rebel, but until that point, we're going to keep having fun with him the way that we know how.

RACHEL BROOKHART

Our American Dream

Growing up together as a family of five was
a choice we made for them and for us.

MY HUSBAND AND I made the decision to raise our three children, Ava, Luka, and Mila, on the road, and we've been traveling the country for a decade.

The National Park Service (NPS) plays a huge part in my children's education: up to this point, our kids have proudly earned 130 Junior Ranger badges. Instead of only reading about Native Americans, my kids visit sacred land to learn their history and their way of living. Instead of only reading about rock formations, glaciers, trees, and wildlife, my kids walk among them. Instead of only reading about Abraham Lincoln, my kids visit his birthplace, run their fingers along the walls of his log cabin, and pay their respects at his burial place. The NPS has been invaluable to my children's education thanks to the knowledge of the park rangers, the educational material the parks provide, and those who fight to keep our public lands available.

There isn't any particular memory I hope my kids will look back on when they are grown, but I hope they will remember that we traded the supposed "American Dream" to carefully carve out our own version. Growing up together

as a family of five was a choice we made for them and for us. In the end, spending time with those who matter is the most important of all.

The other day, someone asked our eight-year-old, Mila, if she remembers living in a house. She shrugged her bare shoulders and shook her head. The kids talk about how someday they will move into a small house and decorate their room with llamas and bunk beds, how they will take dance classes and grow strawberries, too. Every so often we ask the kids if they want to stop traveling and settle down. They tell us that there's too much more to see in the world. So until they say otherwise, we'll just keep driving.

MARLENE LIN

CAMP KITCHEN ESSENTIALS

It's easy to slip into the habit of eating out when you're on the move, but the ability to cook simple, fresh meals in a well-equipped camp kitchen will increase your quality of life on the road. And eating healthy, nourishing foods can lower overall stress levels while traveling and camping (and help you save money).

Often, life on the road works best when it reflects the life you'd want to be living at home. Keep that in mind as you read through this list of basics to stock in your roadtrip camp kitchen:

TO KEEP YOUR FOOD FRESH You'll either want to buy a refrigerator or a cooler. Both have their pros and cons. A 12-volt, energy efficient fridge and freezer keeps your food from spoiling and means you won't have to buy bags of ice. But it's a more expensive investment up front.

A heavy duty cooler is a cheaper option, but is more likely to result in food spoilage and contamination. And you'll have to keep it stocked with ice, which can be inconvenient and costly over time.

TO COOK ON The best camp stoves simulate the experience of cooking at home. Research a classic affordable two burner that's lightweight enough to use in and out of your vehicle (if you are using inside a vehicle, make sure to crack the door and windows before igniting and keep all flammable materials at a safe distance). In a pinch, a single burner or backpacking stove can be a great alternative, especially for a solo traveler. Some include attachments for fry-pans.

TO COOK WITH There are a lot of options for camp kitchen cookware. It's best to keep in mind what cookware you use at home when replicating and downsizing for the road. Consider what meals you like to cook, which vessels can be used to make a variety of meals, and how much storage space you will have in your vehicle. Using cookware that has multiple utilities and vessels that nest within one another can be a great way to save space.

If you're cooking over a campfire, a Dutch Oven is a great way to simulate a real oven. A cast-iron skillet can be used to prepare a range of dishes, and can be placed directly on the grate over a fire. Make sure to keep any vessels used over fire well-seasoned to prevent rusting.

TO EAT AND DRINK WITH Look for durable, lightweight, and compact dining supplies that can be used in a variety of ways (for example, most meals can be eaten out of a bowl so consider leaving your plates behind. And maybe you can drink your coffee and wine out of the same trusty mug). Or, if you have a good deal of storage space, take items from your own kitchen. Above all, take only what your party will need. Odds are you won't be serving dinner for eight on the road.

KITCHEN ACCESSORIES These are items you use at home and while camping: a wooden spoon, cooking knife (bring the knife from home that you're going to miss the most), sponge, pot holder, spatula, cutting board, can opener, cheese grater, kitchen scissors, corkscrew, bottle-opener, and French press, to name a few. Multi-tools—compact devices that include a knife, corkscrew, can opener, bottle opener, and other handy tools—are a great option.

PANTRY ESSENTIALS Just because you're cooking on the road doesn't mean your food can't be interesting. Don't forget to pack pantry essentials like spices, vanilla, sugar, olive oil, hot sauce, and go-to dry goods like oatmeal, flour, and beans (look for instant or quick-cook options to save on cooking gas and time).

TRANSPLANTS

Finding a Connection in the Landscape

I need to feel connected to the landscape I photograph, otherwise it seems to me that my photos mean nothing and are empty of life.

AS LONG AS I CAN REMEMBER, I've been fascinated by Scotland. Growing up in France, I had a romantic and clichéd vision of its history, legends, and stories. They were widely spread in Europe and commonly depicted in the films I loved. I was scared, upon traveling there for the first time, of not finding the Scotland I had imagined, but it was exactly as I had dreamt, and more. I immediately felt as though I were home.

Walking has always been the way I prefer to discover a place. I like to make an effort to reach a point and I also enjoy the slow pace. It's the only way for me to really feel as though I am there, that I am seeing, hearing, feeling the place . . . photography gives me a good excuse to take my time!

I think that photography makes me watch with more care, be more attentive to the details, look for the change in the landscape—sometimes within a

few minutes, just because a cloud is hiding the sun. Photography makes me more aware of a landscape I am evolving in.

I need to feel connected to the landscape I photograph, otherwise it seems to me that my photos mean nothing and are empty of life. The images I make are about the landscape as well as my feelings when seeing it and experiencing it.

Sometimes these emotions can be quite complex or intense, and I feel I need to push my photo toward something visually different, sometimes almost abstract, to render the emotion more adequately. This is, I think, what led me to experiment more.

D'AUSSI LOIN QUE je me souvienne, j'ai toujours été fascinée par l'Écosse. Ayant grandi en France, j'avais cette vision très romantique et pleine de clichés de son histoire et de ses légendes. Tout cela était largement véhiculé en Europe et communément dépeint dans les nombreux films qui ont bercé ma jeunesse! Lors de mon premier voyage ici, j'avais peur de ne pas trouver le pays que j'avais imaginé, mais c'était exactement dans mes rêves et même plus. Je me suis immédiatement sentie à ma place, comme chez moi.

J'ai toujours préféré la marche pour découvrir un lieu. J'aime sa lenteur tout autant que le fait qu'il me soit nécessaire de faire un effort pour atteindre un point donné. La marche est pour moi la seule manière de pleinement "être" à l'endroit où je suis, de vraiment voir, entendre, ressentir un lieu . . . la photographie me donne une bonne excuse pour prendre mon temps!

Je pense que la photo me fait regarder avec plus d'intensité ce qui m'entoure, être plus attentive aux détails, faire attention aux changements dans les paysages—parfois en l'espace de quelques minutes, juste parce qu'un nuage vient cacher le soleil. La photo me rend plus consciente des paysages dans lesquels j'évolue.

J'ai besoin de me sentir connectée aux paysages que je photographie, autrement il me semble que mes photos sont dénuées de sens, vides de toute vie. Les images que je crée évoquent les paysages tout autant que les sentiments que j'éprouve en les parcourant.

Il arrive parfois que ces émotions soient si intenses ou complexes que j'ai alors le besoin de pousser mes photos vers quelque chose de visuellement différent pour pouvoir mieux retranscrire ce que je ressens. C'est ce qui me fait expérimenter de plus en plus et parfois même m'approcher de formes presque abstraites.

VIRGINIE CHABROL

FINDING HOME

Home can be as elusive as your wandering soul. And yet, home is so often the end goal, even the reason for travel. True home is appealing. It's a constant—where we come from or where we wish we came from. Home is a culture and the people who shape it. Home is a memory of warmth for which we'll always be longing.

So, how do we know when we're home? I've heard that you aren't able to put a finger on it until you're there. And you might not be able to open the door and step inside. There is no door to a place as big as Wyoming's Grand Tetons or as infinitely small as moments passing.

We find home on the road. We find it in a return. We crane our necks to look up at it in the towering red cedar and examine its intricate detail on a fallen leaf. It's written in the margins of our grandmother's favorite book.

The beauty of home is if you're open to it, it welcomes you, every time.

Spirited Pursuit

There are places that are deeply connected to my identity.

I WAS BORN IN CAMEROON, AFRICA, but grew up in the United States. I'm currently living a nomadic life after moving back to Africa to explore and document the continent long-term, which forced me to redefine what home actually means. Through this journey, I have learned that home for me is a feeling and I find it mostly in people, not a specific place. With that said, there are places that are deeply connected to my identity: Cameroon for my childhood memories and foundation as a person; the United States for my formative years; and now the road (and Africa in general), where I am currently evolving and becoming.

Africa is in dire need of rebranding and of being captured through inspired eyes. Africa also needs more Africans to tell the world her story. We haven't always been at the center of our own narratives, but that is no longer the case thanks to the digital age. I wanted to be part of the rebrand by sharing my genuine experiences as a solo female traveler throughout the continent to empower and teach both Africans, and the world, how much beauty exists beyond stereotypes.

There are several misconceptions about being a tourist in Africa (including, but not limited to, violence, disease, and theft), which all stem from fear that results from a lack of adequate information. Think about it: does the world only ever see images of the United States represented by Louisiana after Hurricane Katrina or France after the Paris attacks? Is there a travel advisory issued for these countries because of those events? While they are very real and serious issues, they do not adequately represent the narrative of these countries. Through my work as a writer and photographer traveling in Africa, I hope to show the world that the same logic applies when considering travel to African nations.

LEE LITUMBE

A Cure for Homesickness

I needed something to fill the void.
Motorcycles seemed like the next best thing.

I EXPERIENCE HOMESICKNESS like most people experience cravings, if you can imagine a craving plaguing you day and night. The good days are those when I can bury myself in an art piece that reminds me of home. Big skies. Mountains. Open spaces. And a lot of redneck. It helps for a time, but it's really only a placebo.

I'm passionate about my home state of Montana, rural life, and motorcycling. I started riding motorcycles after moving to Portland, Oregon. I figured if I couldn't ride horses as I had in Montana, I needed something to fill the void. Motorcycles seemed like the next best thing. I had no idea how important they would become to me.

When I'm on the bike, I don't think about how much I want to go home. All I think about is the road and the scenery immediately in front of me. I spent my first two years or so riding by myself. I saw it as a great way to get to Montana and back at half the cost of my fuel-guzzling car. The only people I ran into on the road were dudes. I had no idea there was a whole subculture of women motorcyclists until I found TheMotoLady.com.

It was then that I really became inspired to be a part of the moto community and start creating work inspired by it. It is incredible to me how many people in the motorcycling community I've met and had the opportunity to work with because of my drawings of women riding motorcycles. I haven't mastered the art of drawing from memory quite yet, so when I run across a particularly beautiful thing, I always take photographs to draw from when I return home.

AMANDA ZITO

Carving Out a
Home Abroad

Whether it was the turquoise water, the
snow-capped peaks, the green forest, whatever
it was—it came together to enchant me more
than anywhere else I'd been my whole life.

MY LIFE IS FOCUSED ON PLACE and my connection to it. I'm the daughter
of park rangers and we moved a lot. I spent the first six years of my life at
Yosemite National Park and the rest of my childhood spread out across parks
in Texas.

When I was in high school, I thought, "I think I want to do the same
thing as my parents. I want to spend time outside." And in certain ways, my
parents expected that I'd follow in their footsteps. They believed in that lifestyle and wanted that for me.

I started my career in Rocky Mountain National Park in Colorado, but
then I visited New Zealand during a college break. With that visit came a
recognition of a path that I'd never considered before. It consumed me. I was

struck by the landscapes and the people and the easy way of life. I could not believe how big the mountains were or how straight they rose from the low valleys. It all just seemed as close to perfect as I could imagine. Whether it was the turquoise water, the snow-capped peaks, the green forest, whatever it was—it came together to enchant me more than anywhere else I'd been my whole life. It was love. My whole goal became working in New Zealand.

I decided to test out living there for six months. I wanted to work for the Department of Conservation in what I knew best, national parks. As a young girl from the States with a working holiday visa, I had to make myself competitive to the government of New Zealand. I spent the whole summer working toward my goal and ultimately got a position as a hut warden.

After this first season in New Zealand, I got a position at Katmai National Park in Alaska, but my heart was still in New Zealand. When I'd left, I had a feeling of wanting to return, and that feeling always stayed with me. I could either try to bury the feeling or accept it. I decided I wanted to accept it. I had a gut feeling and I wanted to follow it.

I feel like I've built my own career here in New Zealand, separate from my parents. I'm now a biodiversity ranger. I go into the mountains for ten days at a time and work to protect native species. Of course I miss my parents and friends in the States but I believe the distance has helped me become a more active daughter and friend. As far as place is concerned, this is the place for me.

CRYSTAL BRINDLE

ADVOCATES

Taking a Chance on Camping

In the boundless landscapes of this country,
we find our love for a new nationalism.

I FELL IN LOVE with the United States as a child. Born and raised in India, I learned this country the way any eight-year-old child learns anything. I was afraid and excited and fell in love with the wild spaces that lay at the outskirts of my new American life. But even at a young age, I was aware of the fact that I didn't look like the others in the campground or on hiking trails—but I didn't dare wonder why. As new immigrants we often accepted facts as they were presented to us.

My immigrant parents took a chance on camping. They wanted to give us America and so on we went to explore her, with a single tent and a few sleeping bags. We gained wisdom from all the white families around us who didn't smile at us but gave us just enough space to be their neighbors. I remember clearly the moments I lay staring up at the tent ceiling as I fell asleep. A little brown, immigrant girl smiles to herself in a Minnesota campground. Tired from all the newness of the day, she yawns and thinks, "I love America."

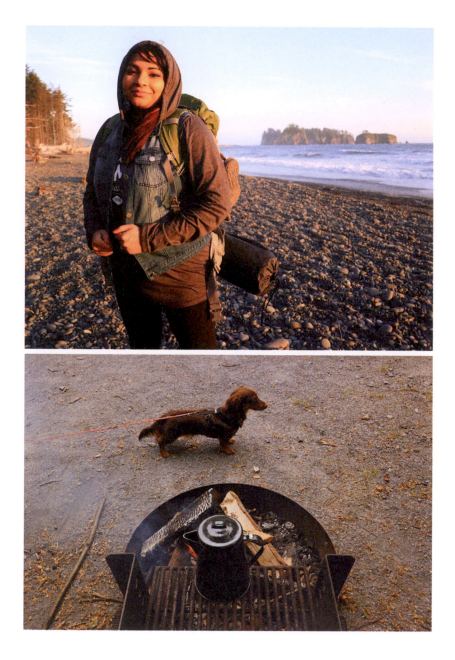

So much has changed since then. I am a grown woman now and no longer the "other" in my immigrant mind. I am the patriotic American I always aspired to become. I am flawed but strong. I am scared for my country's future but unwilling to stop fighting for its betterment. I am a lover of wild spaces and a proponent for sharing their grace with others who haven't had the opportunity to experience them—people whose formative memories may not be scented by dirt and pines and wood smoke and morning dew.

I want every little brown girl and brown boy, and every girl and every boy—whoever doubted their self-worth and sense of belonging in this country—to venture outdoors and explore it with a sense of wonder that comes with this privilege called confidence. I want everyone to stumble across treasures the way I have—in grassy fields, in wooded lands, on snow-covered lakes somewhere out there in "real America." All of America. Out there, in the wild, we make the memories that form us. In the boundless landscapes of this country, we find our love for a new nationalism. One grounded in humility and gratitude and driven by a desire to share, protect, and diversify.

AMBREEN TARIQ

Cerebral Palsy Strong

Anyone who has a disability just wants to be treated like everyone else, even if they walk differently or look differently.

I HAVE CEREBRAL PALSY (CP), a physical disability that affects the left side of my body. My brain can't tell my muscles to relax, so I'm constantly locked up. I have this amazing device called the ExoSym™ that helps me get around more easily.

My parents were told I might never be able to walk at all, but I worked hard to keep up with my athletic family. My identical twin sister doesn't have CP. I've always had the mentality that *I can do everything you can do, maybe just a little bit slower.* Language is so important when you talk to a child with CP; you're telling them either "you can do it" or "you can't."

On long hikes, my legs get really fatigued. A lot of people ask if I'm okay, but I try to normalize the way I am as much as I can. I think at the end of the day, anyone who has a disability just wants to be treated like everyone else, even if they walk differently or look differently. They should be treated with the same regard and understanding.

People have asked me, "How are you so open about your CP?" I don't feel like I have a choice. I think that if I were to hide that side of myself, I wouldn't feel happy and whole. I like to encourage other people to be who they are without reservations. I want other people to know that it's good to be intentional, too, and think about what they want to do and achieve.

KATY FETTERS

HOW TO TELL YOUR STORY

If you want to engage with the outdoor space, not simply recreate, there's value in storytelling. The key is to strike the right balance between sharing your story and listening to and amplifying the stories of others.

SHARE There's a difference between talking about yourself and leading by example. Sharing your story need not be rooted in narcissism, but representation and connection. There has typically been a narrow range of experiences that has dominated our narratives about the outdoors. You should share your own story, because the same old tales can be told for only so long around the campfire. New stories are an opportunity to bond, engage, and ignite dialogue and connection. If you write a poem about the anxiety (and excitement!) you felt on the knife edge of Mount Katahdin and you share it with a friend and she gets it, your story grows.

LISTEN We all want to see ourselves reflected in others. We want to see ourselves in the media we consume and the spaces we inhabit. The outdoors is no different. For the last few years, women and nonbinary folk and fat people and Indigenous cultures and immigrants and people of color have been screaming, "We're here!" Make sure you listen to and consider the experiences that may not be your own.

AMPLIFY Don't stop at telling your own story, amplify others. Take the little stool you've been standing on and pass it along. Search outside of yourself to discover *what it takes* to support what you believe in, and do it with all your heart.

Fat Girls Hiking

I identify as fat as a way to reclaim the word, to give it a positive power.

BEING FAT ON THE TRAIL comes with stereotypes. People assume I hike to lose weight or that I'm a beginner, and say, "Good for you! You're almost to the top!" I wonder if they say that to thin people, too? Or people who "look the part" of what a hiker is "supposed" to be? This happens often on popular trails I frequent near Portland, especially hard paths with a lot of elevation gain. It's frustrating that these assumptions exist, but I don't need or seek others' approval. I hike for myself.

The word *fat* is typically used as a negative slur to shame people with bigger bodies. It's been used as an insult to harm me my whole life. It's true, I'm FAT. I identify as fat as a way to reclaim the word, to give it a positive power. When we stop thinking of fat as bad, we look at ourselves and others in a light that allows them to just be people with varying-size bodies.

I founded Fat Girls Hiking in 2015. I was hiking a lot and using social media to share my photos. At the time, there were no outdoor Instagram accounts representing and celebrating people of varying sizes, races, genders, ages, and classes. I wanted to fill some of that gap. What started as an Instagram account quickly turned into a desire to create an outdoor community

where we can not only hike together, but also build friendships and support one another.

The mission of Fat Girls Hiking is to provide a space where we can show up as we are and be accepted. We want to take the shame and stigma out of the word *fat* and empower it. Our motto, "Trails Not Scales," focuses on self-care.

I've had people who had never been hiking come to a group hike and say, "You changed my life." Encouraging people to show up as they are and accepting them for what they are capable of is empowering!

When we break down the barriers, we make the outdoors more accessible. People often tell me that they get left behind on the trail when hiking with other groups. Fat Girls Hiking leaves no hikers behind. When we include people who hike at differing paces, we create a space that is welcoming to all. When we feel welcomed, we are more likely to participate in that activity, build community around it, and pass on a love of the outdoors to others.

SUMMER

Cultivating Change

I'm advocating to make outdoor arenas reflect
the diverse makeup of the United States.

I ABSOLUTELY LOVE the Avenue of the Giants in Northern California. There is such beauty and tranquility there. I can sit for hours gazing at those gentle giants, the redwood trees. Every turn along the twenty-plus-mile drive brings wonders and anticipation of what natural sculpture will jump out at you next. There are so many hiking trails and campsites in the area, I could spend days and not touch 5 percent of the open spaces. This is my happy place. The reason I work to increase diversity and inclusion in the outdoor industry is twofold. First and foremost, my motivation is to engage audiences in hopes of cultivating new stewards of the great outdoors. We need more faces—*new* faces—to fight for the protection of our public lands. Second, people of color are in these spaces, but you would never know by their absence in outdoor magazines and the social media feeds of outdoor retailers. I'm advocating to make outdoor arenas reflect the diverse makeup of the United States. We, too, belong and it's time that message is projected in marketing campaigns and publications.

Outdoor spaces lend themselves to conversations that can cultivate change and a stronger sense of self. When we gather in these spaces to have

conversations, black, brown, and white individuals alike are soothed by the calmness of our surroundings. I think it is in those moments that we understand the importance of gathering, to experience our differences and our likeness and to have these difficult conversations, in hopes of them leading to a greater understanding of our purpose and obligation to the land.

I live in debt to those who came before me and in obligation to those who will come after. What better way to honor both than fighting for equal acknowledgment in outdoor spaces.

TERESA BAKER

RESPECTFUL RECREATION

Getting outside is a release for us all. And with that liberation comes the responsibility of respectful recreation. Here're a few tips on remaining respectful in the outdoors:

PRACTICE "LEAVE NO TRACE" PRINCIPLES The nonprofit organization Leave No Trace (LNT) details excellent guidelines for minimizing your impact while enjoying outdoor spaces. If you spend time in the outdoors, you should give LNT a comprehensive read.

BRUSH UP ON YOUR TRAIL ETIQUETTE Being respectful in the outdoors doesn't mean just treating the land properly, but other people, too. Remember to yield to those coming up the trail, don't be afraid to say hello, and recognize that you're not alone out there. Keep outside voices (or music) to a respectful level for other people and animals alike.

READ UP Familiarize yourself with local laws, ordinances, and customs that may impact you. Is it wildfire season? Is there trail maintenance that might divert your planned route? Knowing beforehand will make for a more considered experience.

LEARN SOME HISTORY Context lends a more meaningful depth to your time outdoors. Is your favorite park a historical farm that was donated to the community? What's the Indigenous name of the mountain you're climbing? Did Buffalo Soldiers play a pivotal role in a battle on the land you're crossing? You might be surprised what you see in the land you play on.

ACT LIKE A LOCAL While you may be simply passing through, the locals use the land year in and year out. Be respectful of their spaces and be open to their words of advice.

KEEP PETS ON A LEASH While we trust our pets implicitly and know their personalities better than anyone, not everyone else does, and that's okay. Keeping your pets on a leash and being respectful gives pet owners a good reputation and helps keep public spaces accessible for pets in the future.

CONSIDER BEFORE YOU POST We all want to share the incredible places that inspire us. The double-edged sword is that overexposure on social media can lead to a negative impact on a beautiful place that doesn't have the proper infrastructure to handle its newfound fame. Sometimes those secret spots that were hard to find should stay that way. A little surprise in the world is welcome.

Wild and
Weightless

You prove to yourself and others
that you are stronger than the negative
thoughts in your head.

WILD AND WEIGHTLESS sprang from a moment of clarity I had while walking down the trail to Conundrum Hot Springs in Colorado. I had fled Denver to escape the anxiety, emptiness, and disconnect I was feeling in the city. My past eating disorder behaviors and thoughts were reappearing, and I was losing my sense of self that I had found being outside. I looked in the mirror and thought only about how I wanted my reflection to be different. Sometimes I was too ashamed to look in the mirror at all.

Once I was on the trail, I felt a sense of calm, reassurance, and appreciation. I was reminded of the love I have for my body, which has taken me to the top of mountains and through countless National Parks, trails, beaches, and foreign countries. My body has been with me in my lowest moments and has survived the abuse I put it through. I wondered if other women were going outdoors because that is where they felt strength and freedom from disordered

eating. A week later I created Wild and Weightless, an Instagram account with a mission to bring us together.

Although eating disorders are extremely isolating, by telling your story, you take back some of the control that eating disorders erode. You prove to yourself and others that you are stronger than the negative thoughts in your head. This can be scary, but having a community of people supporting your journey makes it easier.

When you are camping, most thoughts focus around strategy and survival. "What do I have to do to stay warm tonight?" or "How do I safely get from point A to point B?" This promotes self-efficacy and self-care. People who struggle with eating disorders are not very good at taking care of themselves. Outdoor activities like skiing, climbing, rafting, or whatever your passion may be take a lot of positive self-talk. "You got this," "You are strong," "Go for it." We can bring these phrases back to our daily lives by spending time outdoors.

I've hiked thirty peaks to raise awareness for the thirty million people who currently suffer from eating disorders in the United States. I used the donations to transform Wild and Weightless into a nonprofit that offers outdoor trips for those touched by eating disorders.

Bring awareness to what makes you the happiest. Are there ever times when you are having so much fun that you don't think about what you look like or what you are putting in your mouth? For me, it's when I'm skiing. Find your happy thing, and do it more. It could be what saves you.

KRISTEN ALES

A Long View

My fondest memories are with the
people that I met on trail.

I SPENT ALL OF MY TWENTIES not really sure what I was passionate about. When I finally figured out what it was, I had to go for it and make it a long-term goal. I wanted to do something that would challenge me physically and mentally for a long period of time. I wanted to build resilience in my lowest moments and tell myself that any discomfort was only temporary. Hiking the Pacific Crest Trail (PCT) was perfect for me in that season of life. I discovered that I truly love walking all day. As an early riser, there is nothing I enjoyed more than getting up each morning in the dark and watching the sun rise as I walked along a ridgeline. My fondest memories are with the people that I met on trail. They were complete strangers in the beginning who became like family in just a few days.

I do not want to thru-hike every year, because I want to spend my time directly helping the trail itself. I was living a very self-centered life preparing for, during, and after my hike. I felt I got what I "needed" from the PCT, but now, I want to volunteer trail maintenance, spread awareness to protect the trail, and educate youth about the outdoors. In the long run, I just want to be living a meaningful life that improves the lives of others.

KAREN K. WANG

Speaking for the Outdoors

We're all looking for the next thing
to move us and shake us, and for me,
that thing was outdoor advocacy.

I WORK IN OUTDOOR ADVOCACY, and in my proverbial toolbox you'll find social media, content creation, community organizing, and digital marketing. Most of my work is in the digital space, but my greatest joy is when my work leaves the Internet and galvanizes the outdoor community into real-world action. It's all rooted in my years spent creating content, writing, documenting trips, and sharing my stories on the road. I can't pinpoint the moment I became "a voice for outdoor advocacy," but it was the result of following meaningful projects and work opportunities. We're all looking for the next thing to move us and shake us, and for me, that thing was outdoor advocacy—and my strongest medium is social media. Finding and using your voice is essential. We simply must take action on the issues that matter most to us, from public lands to women's health.

Utah is my home. I was drawn here during my first cross-country climbing trip and it took me six years of return visits to settle down permanently. I'm enamored with its southern desert, the climbing, the easy access to the outdoors, the strong community here, and of course, the challenging political terrain. I wanted to live in a place where my work is important, and public lands are particularly threatened in Utah.

If I ever have a daughter, I hope she, too, will one day jump in a truck with her girlfriends to meander down dirt roads, watching red dust collect on her feet and a sunburn slowly creeping across her desert skin.

KATIE BOUÉ

THANKS

When I launched She-Explores.com, I wrote, "she isn't me," and that statement is still true today. In completing this book, I have to acknowledge the hundreds of women who have contributed their writing, photography, artwork, and voices to She-Explores.com, our social media handles, our podcasts, and this book. Some early contributors come to mind: Alison Turner, Kit Whistler, Brooke Weeber, Kat Carney, Charley Zheng, Kristen Blanton, and Madison Perrins, among many others; thank you for the willingness to trust your work and words on an unknown platform.

In the past four years, I've had countless advocates, collaborators, and mentors. I'm hugely grateful to Liz Song Mandell for our long conversations, Jeanine Pesce for sharing her knowledge, Jessie Davis and Julie Hotz for collaborating on a film project, Ashlee Langholz for helping said film come to life, and Steve Wilson for encouraging me to start a podcast. Thank you to Sara Murphy and Sydney Halle for their consistent support. Thanks to Sarah Menzies and Anna Brones for their good humor and ridiculous text message chains. Thank you to Laura Hughes, Hailey Hirst, Stephanie Wright, Leslie Schipper, Dani Opal, Korrin Bishop, and Jaymie Shearer for dedicating their time and creative energy over the years.

Thank you to the team at Chronicle Books, especially my editor Rachel Hiles, for her excitement about this project and her keen eye for detail.

Thank you to my parents, Mary and Tom Straub, for cultivating a quiet curiosity in all things. Thank you to my aunt, Katie Matthews, for the potential she finds in abstractions. Thank you to my brother, Matt Straub, and his family, who help me look at the bright side. And of the many no longer with us: Rosemary Kelleher ("Grammar") and James Kelleher ("Uncle Jim"): the former for teaching me to not just get lost in novels, but to analyze them; the latter for knowing that historical landmarks are best paired with ice cream cones.

Thank you to Jon Gaffney for always being up for a brainstorm, road trip, plane flight, or night in playing cribbage. Life is more fun with you.

And thank you to my twister (twin sister), Lora Straub, for lending her enviable editing skills to this work, her unconditional friendship, and for being my very first tentmate.

CONTRIBUTORS

KRISTEN ALES
Instagram: @wildandweightless
& @kales.tales
Website: www.wildandweightless.com

ANASTASIA M. ALLISON
Instagram: @anastasia.allison & @
themusicalmountaineers
Website: www.anastasiaallison.com

SARAH ATTAR
Instagram: @sarahattar
Website: www.sarahattar.com

TERESA BAKER
Instagram: @teresabaker11
Facebook: www.facebook.com/
African-American-Nature-Parks-
Experience-355974594517522/

BROOKLYN BELL
Instagram: @badgal_brooky
Website: www.brooklynbelldesign.com

CÉCILE BERTRAND
Instagram: @radiusandulna
Website: www.radius-ulna.com

KATIE BOUÉ
Instagram: @katieboue

CRYSTAL BRINDLE
Instagram: @crystalann_b
Website: www.inpursuitofthewild.com

RACHEL BROOKHART
Instagram: @dieselpowerwolfpack

MORGAN BROWN
Instagram: @morgabob
Website: www.deathdialogue.com

IMOGENE CANCELLARE
Instagram: @biologistimogene
Website: www.biologistimogene.com

VIRGINIE CHABROL
Instagram: @louiseoupas
Website: www.lp1n.com

MARINEL MALVAR DE JESUS
Instagram: @browngaltrekker
Website: www.browngaltrekker.com

ELLYSA EVANS
Instagram: @graceandgravity

KATY FETTERS
Instagram: @cerebralpalsystrong

ROSE FREEMAN
Instagram: @missroselouise &
@themusicalmountaineers

MARYELLEN HACKETT
Instagram: @hereandfarther
Website: www.hereandfarther.com

SHANTI HODGES
Instagram: @hikingmyway
Website: www.hikeitbaby.com,
www.hikingmyway.com

JULIE A. HOTZ
Instagram: @julieahotz
Website: www.julieahotz.com

KATHY KARLO
Instagram: @inheadlights
Website: www.fortheloveofclimbing.com

PARIS LEE
Instagram: @novelkulture
Website: www.youtube.com/
novelkulture

SAM LEE
Instagram: @samleehello
Website: www.samleehello.com

MARLENE LIN
Instagram: @mali.mish
Website: www.malimish.com

LEE LITUMBE
Instagram: @spiritedpursuit
Website: www.spiritedpursuit.com

SIMONE MARTIN-NEWBERRY
Website: www.darkerthangreen.com

AMANDA MONTHEI
Instagram: @a_monthei

MADISON PERRINS
Instagram: @madisonperrins
Website: www.mperrins.com

GRETCHEN POWERS
Instagram: @gpowersfilm
Website: www.gpowersfilm.com

NOËL RUSSELL
Instagram: @noel_russ

AMANDA SANDLIN
Instagram: @amandsandlin
Website: www.amandasandlin.com

SUMMER
Instagram: @fatgirlshiking
Website: www.fatgirlshiking.com

AMBREEN TARIQ
Instagram: @brownpeoplecamping
Website: www.brownpeoplecamping.com

ASHLEIGH THOMPSON
Instagram: @ashanishinaabe

AGNES VIANZON
Website: www.easternsierracc.org

KAREN K. WANG
Instagram: @karenkwang
Website: www.karenkwang.com

CAITLIN WARD
Instagram: @picnicsincoolplaces
and @caitward12

BROOKE WEEBER
Instagram: @brooke_weeber
Website: ww.thelittlecanoe.com

IRENE YEE
Instagram: @ladylockoff
Website: www.ladylockoff.com

AMANDA ZITO
Instagram: @blindthistle

CREDITS

Page 144: Photograph copyright © 2017 Ellysa Evans

Page 146: Photograph copyright © 2017 Morgan Brown

Page 148-149 (clockwise from top left): Photograph copyright © 2017 Morgan Brown, www.instagram.com/morgabob; photograph copyright © 2017 Mackenzie Duncan, www.instagram.com/themackenzielife; photograph copyright © 2017 Morgan Brown

Page 150: Photograph copyright © 2017 Noël Russell

Page 153-155: Photographs copyright © 2017 Noël Russell

Page 157-160: Photographs copyright © 2017 Gale Straub

Page 162: Photograph copyright © 2017 Rachel Brookhart

Page 164-165: Photographs copyright © 2017 Rachel Brookhart

Page 166: Photograph copyright © 2017 Mali Mish, www.malimish.com

Page 168-169: Photographs copyright © 2017. Mali Mish, www.malimish.com

Pages 171: Photograph copyright © 2017 Gale Straub

Page 174-175: Photograph copyright © 2017 Crystal Brindle

Page 176: Photograph copyright © 2017 Virginie Chabrol

Page 177: Photograph copyright © 2017 Crystal Brindle

Pages 178: Photograph copyright © 2017 Virginie Chabrol

Pages 180-181: Photograph copyright © 2017 Virginie Chabrol

Page 183: Photograph copyright © 2017 Gale Straub

Page 184: Photograph copyright © 2017 Lee Litumbe/Spirited Pursuit, www.spiritedpursuit.com

Page 186: Photograph copyright © 2017 Lee Litumbe/Spirited Pursuit, www.spiritedpursuit.com

Page 188: Photograph © 2017 Amanda Zito

Page 190: Artwork copyright © 2017 Amanda Zito, www.instagram.com/blindthistle

Page 191: Top photograph © 2017 Gale Straub; bottom photograph and artwork © 2017 Amanda Zito

Page 192: Photograph copyright © 2017 Danilo Hegg, www.southernalpsphotography.com

Pages 194-195: Photograph copyright © 2017 Crystal Brindle

Page 196: Photograph copyright © 2017 Danilo Hegg, www.southernalpsphotography.com

Page 200-201: Photograph copyright © 2017 Karen K. Wang

Page 202: Photograph copyright © 2017 Karen K. Wang

Page 203: Photograph copyright © 2014 Gale Straub

Page 204: Photograph copyright © 2017 Ambreen Tariq

Page 206: Photographs copyright © 2017 Ambreen Tariq

Page 208: Photograph copyright © 2017 Blnk Films, www.instagram.com/blnkfilms

Page 210: Photograph copyright © 2017 Blnk Films, www.instagram.com/blnkfilms

Page 213: Photograph copyright © 2016 Gale Straub

Page 214: Photograph provided by Summer, www.fatgirlshiking.com

Page 216: Photograph provided by Summer, www.fatgirlshiking.com

Pages 218-219: Photograph copyright © 2017 Gale Straub

Page 220: Photograph copyright © 2017 Teresa Baker

Page 222: Photograph copyright © 2017 Victoria Reeder

Page 225-227: Photographs copyright © 2017 Gale Straub

Page 228: Photograph copyright © Kristen Ales

Page 230: Photograph copyright © Kristen Ales

Page 232: Photograph copyright © 2017 Karen K. Wang

Page 235-236: Photographs copyright © 2017 Katherine Boué

PEOPLE PICTURED

Page 10 (left): Photograph of Julie A. Hotz

Page 13: Photograph of Lindsay Hollinger

Page 16 (top): Photograph of Kristen Ales

Page 16 (bottom right): From left to right: Photograph of Lisa Bernadin and Gretchen Powers

Page 16 (bottom left): Photograph of Brooklyn Bell

Pages 26-27: From left to right: Julie A. Hotz and Kristen Rapinchuk

Page 28 (top): Photograph of Kristen Rapinchuk

Page 28 (bottom): Photograph of Gale Straub

Page 29: Photograph of Amelia Card

Page 45: Photograph of Lisa Bernadin

Page 46 (top and bottom): Photographs of Lisa R. Bernadin and Gretchen Powers

Page 60 (top): Photograph of Jules Davies

Page 60 (bottom): Photograph of Nicole Mills

Page 77 (top): Photograph of Alyx Schwarz

Page 82: Photograph of Brianna Boney

Page 84: Photograph of Diane Wilson

Page 94 (bottom): Photograph of Jessica Speich, Diana Lopez, Yvonnette Quintanilla, Valerie McCampbell, Jamie Shin, Cassee McGann

Page 95: Photograph of MaryEllen Hackett

Page 104 (right): Photograph of Megan Bilby, pictured with Shanti Hodges

Page 106 (left): Photograph of Megan Bilby, pictured with Shanti Hodges

Page 111: From left to right: Photograph of Amelia Card and Julie A. Hotz

Page 136 (bottom left): Photograph of Mali Mish kids

Page 183: Photograph of Liv Combe

Page 200-201: Photograph of Karen K. Wang

Page 227: Photograph of Kristin Rapinchuk